Literature and Drama

CONCEPTS OF LITERATURE

GENERAL EDITOR: WILLIAM RIGHTER

Department of English
University of Warwick

Volumes in this series include

COMPARATIVE LITERATURE Henry Gifford,
University of Bristol

STYLE AND STYLISTICS Graham Hough,
University of Cambridge

Literature and Drama

with special reference to Shakespeare and his contemporaries

by Stanley Wells

The Shakespeare Institute
Stratford-upon-Avon

LONDON
ROUTLEDGE & KEGAN PAUL

First published in 1970
by Routledge & Kegan Paul Ltd
Broadway House, 68-74 Carter Lane
London E.C.4
Printed in Great Britain
by Northumberland Press Limited
Gateshead
© Stanley Wells 1970
No part of this book may be reproduced
in any form without permission from
the publisher, except for the quotation
of brief passages in criticism

ISBN 0 7100 6909 X (C)
ISBN 0 7100 6910 3 (P)

Eng drama

PR
623
W4
1970

105345

General Editor's Introduction

The study of literature has normally centred on the consideration of work, author, or historical period. But increasingly there is a demand for a more analytic approach, for investigation and explanation of literary concepts of crucial ideas and issues—topics which are of general importance to the critical consideration of particular works. This series undertakes to provide a clear description and critical evaluation of such important ideas as 'symbolism', 'realism', 'style' and other terms used in literary discussion. It also undertakes to define the relationship of literature to other intellectual disciplines: anthropology, philosophy, psychology, etc., for it is in connection with such related fields that much important recent critical work has been done. *Concepts of Literature* will both account for the methodology of literary study, and will define its dimensions by reference to the many activities that throw light upon it. Individual works will describe the fundamental outlines of particular problems and explore the frontiers that they suggest. The series as a whole will provide a survey of recent literary thought.

One of the great discoveries of the modern theatre is the multiplicity of relationship between the text of a play and its presence on the stage, between the literary and the theatrical experience. And behind this lies both the historical rediscovery of theatrical forms that are not primarily literary, and the historical consciousness of how the pre-suppositions of a period may subtly alter the meanings of even the most familiar text. Dr Wells approaches these problems through the works of Shakespeare and his con-temporaries. The earliest printed plays, which existed in a context of non-dramatic entertainment, also established the duality of role of the play for public performance and for the individual reader's pleasure. The Masque shows the ex-treme of disproportion between a literary skeleton and the theatrical means that give it life. And it is perhaps with respect to the theatre of Shakespeare that we have best understood the powers of both actor and director to inter-pret and transform. Dr Wells uses his study of recent pro-ductions to examine the freedom and responsibility which such powers imply; he is concerned with the claims to autonomy of literary text and of the world of the play, and with what the critic learns from their subtle interplay.

WILLIAM RIGHTER

Contents

Foreword

Most drama has some literary quality, and most dramatic scripts can give literary pleasure when read, but the reading of a play is a necessarily incomplete experience. This book attempts both to illustrate this statement and to explore some of its implications. Because the greatest English drama was written in the sixteenth and seventeenth centuries, most of the illustrations are taken from works of that time, but the topic is relevant to any period. Some modern dramatists very obviously work along with their medium, rarely indulging in the set piece that might be considered expressive in its own right. Harold Pinter is an obvious example of a writer who leaves much unsaid: or leaves it to be said in between the lines. Yet the technique is not new, and can indeed be traced in plays of many periods: in Chekov's, for instance, or in Shakespeare's, notably in scenes such as those in Justice Shallow's orchard in *Henry IV, Part Two*. So Chapter One of this book looks at some of the areas of plays that are dependent on the art of the theatre, and points to the fluidity of interpretation to which this gives rise. The following two chapters investigate more specialized areas. Chapter Two looks at the history of the printing of plays and the surprisingly limited attempts that have been made to convey the theatrical experience. Chapter Three develops the theme by considering a particular example of a printed text—Ben Jonson's masque *Pleasure Reconciled to Virtue*—and comparing the experience of reading it with that suggested by contemporary accounts of the work in performance. Finally, Chapter Four moves back to the more general aspects of the topic, considering how the problems created by the instability of theatrical art both affect the criticism of plays and create problems for their theatrical interpreters.

1

Plays as blueprints for performance

Drama in the theatre and the study

The aim of this book is to explore something of the area that lies between the two very different experiences of reading plays and seeing them performed. The difference is liable to be felt in all kinds of dramatic literature, though its critical implications are most acute in relation to plays that have acquired classic status: those that are read and studied as literary objects, for their poetic quality or their quasi-philosophical content, rather than experienced primarily in the theatre. For English-speaking people this means Shakespeare above all, especially now that knowledge and understanding of some of his plays are regarded as a necessary basis of a literary education. For a long time those who study Shakespeare mainly as literature have been urged that he can be truly experienced only in the theatre. They have been reminded that to read a play is an artificial experience, and an incomplete one, akin to reading the score of an orchestral composition without hearing the sounds that it symbolizes. And those who, on the other hand, perform the plays have been admonished for not reading enough of and about Shakespeare. They are told that the experience they provide is not the truly Shakespearian one either, that the plays are commonly distorted by, for instance, the falsity of theatre tradition, the vanity of actors and directors, the need for box-office appeal, and the urge for novelty. It is commonly felt that while theatrical experience of the plays is indispensable to our understanding, it is rarely if ever completely satisfying; that when we return to the printed text we find it suggesting a potentially richer and more complex experience than the theatre has provided.

Nor is this true only of Shakespeare. The problem may seem more acute in relation to poetic than to prose drama. Poetry in its richness of expression may seem less dependent on the actor's art than prose, and thus to be more fully satisfying on the printed page; and also, because poetry demands more from the actor than prose, it may seem less likely to be adequately realized in performance. But we know too that modern prose plays reveal different aspects of themselves in the study and in the theatre. Some of Shaw's plays have lately been seen to be far more stage-worthy than we remembered; having found certain modern plays memorable in the theatre, we may have been disappointed to find how little of the excitement was conveyed by the text alone.

Conversely, some writings in dramatic form seem to offer far more to the reader than to the spectator. Some, indeed, do not even ask to be performed : we may think of Shelley's *Prometheus Unbound*, or of Hardy's *The Dynasts*. Others, though they could be acted, seem to ask rather to be read. We think of Milton's *Comus* and *Samson Agonistes*, of Matthew Arnold's *Empedocles on Etna*, or of Byron's plays such as *Manfred* or *Marino Faliero*. Some of these works are occasionally performed, but we do not attend them with lively expectations of theatrical pleasure. Rightly or wrongly, we fear that, for instance, the long speeches of *Comus* will give less pleasure on the stage, where we expect movement and action, than on the page. Milton, too, seems to have felt this, since there are variations between the text as performed and as printed.

Some writers of this kind of play wrote hoping for performance, but seem to have miscalculated their talents. Others wrote specifically to be read, but were sometimes harried into performance. Byron, for instance, writes in the Preface to *Marino Faliero*:

> I have had no view to the stage; in its present state
> it is, perhaps, not a very exalted object of ambition;
> besides, I have been too much behind the scenes
> to have thought it so at any time. And I cannot
> conceive any man of irritable feeling putting
> himself at the mercies of an audience. The sneering
> reader, and the loud critic, and the tart review, are
> scattered and distant calamities; but the trampling
> of an intelligent or of an ignorant audience on a
> production which, be it good or bad, has been a
> mental labour to the writer, is a palpable and
> immediate grievance, heightened by a man's doubt
> of their competency to judge, and his certainty of
> his own imprudence in electing them his judges.
> Were I capable of writing a play which could be
> deemed stage-worthy, success would give me no
> pleasure, and failure great pain.

In fact, to Byron's annoyance, *Marino Faliero* was played at Drury Lane; but he had chosen to write a piece in dramatic form, and with no more by way of stage directions than is necessary for performance, while intending it (as he claimed) simply to be read.

The hazards of performance

This at least leaves the final judgment with the reader. But any play intended for performance raises serious critical problems. How, it may be asked, can we possibly judge a play if we never truly experience it? We cannot appreciate *Hamlet* on the printed page, because it cries out for theatrical realization. Point after point can be taken only in the theatre, conveyed to us by the surges and pauses of the stage action, the physical realization of character only hinted at by the text, the mastery with which the actor of Hamlet plays upon our nerves and senses, our awareness of his silent presence in the rich and formal setting of the first court scene, the interplay among the silent faces that watch his behaviour in the play scene, the timing with which the actors playing the grave-diggers deliver their witticisms, the pathetic appearance of the young and crazed Ophelia singing her fragments of old tunes to her silent auditors.

The effect of the play in performance depends partly on the audience, too; for theatre is a communal activity. Only mad King Ludwig wished to form an audience by himself. When we sit in momentary silence at the conclusion of a tragedy, part of the impressive quality of the experience derives from the fact that hundreds of others are felt to be sharing our emotion. Our laughter during a comedy is far more hearty if the theatre is full than if the audience is thinly scattered over the floor of the house.

Perhaps, then, we should abandon our literary pretensions. Perhaps we should accept the fact that plays are meant to be acted, and enjoy and study them only in the theatre, where they belong. We do not hope to be able to read a symphony as if it were only a pattern of sounds. We know that the pattern is one also of tone colours, that the fact that one line of melody is given to a clarinet instead of an oboe matters, that a solo violin makes a different sound from twenty violins playing in unison. The music exists only in performance, and should be experienced as sound, not as notes in a printed score. But there is a complication. We know too that interpretations vary, that different conductors will produce different effects even with the same music played by the same orchestra; that minute variations of tempo, of balance, of rhythmic emphasis may make all the difference between a dull performance and an exciting one. Each time a piece of music is played it is, at least slightly, a different piece.

The same is true of a play. Each production of it that we see makes it a different play. This is true even of a modern play, even from one performance to the next. An actor fluffs a line, the timing goes wrong: the tension is broken. A member of the audience arrives late or laughs in the wrong place: an effect is lost. An actor is in unusually good form, the house is full, the audience exceptionally responsive: the scene goes better than ever before. How much more acute is the situation with an old play. *Hamlet* again provides a convenient example. The number of variables that are possible is infinite. First, and perhaps most serious of all, is the text. There are two basic problems. The first is that nobody knows what the text of *Hamlet* should be; even, indeed, whether Shakespeare himself ever arrived at a final text. The play survives in an obviously corrupt version known as the Bad Quarto; in a much better one, known as the Good Quarto; and in another, rather different good one, printed in the First Folio. Each includes passages not printed in the others, as well as differences in points of detail within passages common to all versions. Current editions are based on either the Good Quarto or the First Folio, in either case with modifications from the other, and some slight influence from the Bad Quarto. Editors differ in their judgment of the relative merits of these texts. The result is that comparison of, for instance, the New Cambridge, the Signet, and the New Temple editions reveals a number of differences. And in three productions, one based on each of these editions, somewhat different words will be spoken. The differences may not be startling; but they will be there. This critical complication, however, may be regarded as accidental. It is serious in regard to *Hamlet* and to a number of other plays, but it is not a necessary result of the tension between the arts of literature and the theatre.

The second major textual problem standing in the way of an adequate theatrical experience of *Hamlet* is a more inherent one. It derives from the fact that when the play is presented in the modern theatre it is almost always, for one reason or another, and to varying extents, adapted. We do not hear all the words even as decided upon by one editor. The play is extremely long. Its language is archaic and often difficult. It is being presented on a stage of different size and design from the one for which it was written. For these and many other reasons, passages are likely to be omitted. There may be some rewriting, either to simplify or to 'improve' the original. The order of speeches, or even of scenes, may be altered.

Though the words are often altered, they are among the more constant features of productions of old plays. The variety of circumstances in which they are spoken is likely to create an equal variety of effect. A young actor, playing Hamlet, perhaps in modern dress, sounds and looks very different from an older man with a different kind of vocal training and perhaps wearing Elizabethan costume. The play is likely to be presented with sets, costumes, and incidental music varying from one theatre to another. The ages of the actors will vary; so will the pace, the methods of the staging, the lighting effects. Different producers are likely to have different ideas about the play, to be attempting to impose different interpretations.

These circumstances may appear, in the case of a play such as *Hamlet*, to be largely the result of historical circumstance. The play was written centuries ago. Information about its original staging does not survive. Theatrical conditions have changed. We do not know in precisely what costumes it was performed, how old the actors were, whether characters were sometimes on stage at moments when the dialogue does not absolutely require them to be there. So it is worth stressing that the script of any play is likely to invite flexibility of interpretation, that theatre is an intensely imprecise medium. Some dramatists seem to exploit this, others to fight against it. But no matter how detailed the instructions a playwright may give—let him be not only the writer of the play but also the producer, the designer of the sets and costumes, the composer of the music, the choreographer—he remains a participant in an essentially collaborative act. The hints that he gives have to be transmitted to the audience by people other than himself. Other human beings come between his creative effort and the experience of the audience. They may dull it, or they may sharpen it. They may be inefficient transmitters, or they may themselves bring to their roles a creative capacity, making it impossible for us to distinguish between the achievements of the writer and of the actor.

The actor's contribution

An actor is not a passive instrument on which the play-wright plays his tunes. At times the playwright deliber-ately leaves something to him. To take a simple instance from *Hamlet*, the duel scene depends a good deal on the ability of the actors to create the right kind of excitement. If Shakespeare had been writing a novel, the responsibility for controlling his readers' reactions would have been his own; he would have done it through the power of his narrative writing. As he is writing a play, he can only hope that his actors will realize his intentions. And there is always the possibility that an actor will do more. Lines of no literary pretensions may be among the most theatrically effective. John Russell Brown has suggested, for instance, that in *Henry IV, Part Two*

> the crucial moment in the last long interview between
> the dying king and Prince Hal is the simple, incomplete
> verse-line, 'O my son' (IV. iv. 178), which every
> actor of the role in my experience has made more
> affecting than the other hundred and fifty lines of
> the duologue. *Hamlet* has many such lines: 'Go on;
> I'll follow thee' to the Ghost, and 'O God!',
> 'Murder!', 'My uncle!' (I. iv. 79 and 86, and I. v.
> 24 ff.) When Hamlet first calls the Ghost 'father'
> many actors have found that the text asks for
> particular emphasis.

Professor Brown then quotes from Arthur Colby Sprague's *Shakespeare and the Actors*: 'Kean, we are told, was no longer frightened. Booth "dropped on one knee ... and bowed his head, not in terror, but in awe and love". At the sight of the spirit, Salvini's face was "illumined with an awe-struck joy", and his Hamlet "spontaneously, and one would almost say unconsciously, uncovers his head".'

As will be clear from these quotations, it is difficult to draw the line between moments when the actor is interpreting, transmitting, giving full value to something implicit in the text, which can therefore be credited to the author, and other moments when he is adding to it. We may feel that the incomplete verse-line, 'O my son', is obviously designed by Shakespeare to have an intense emotional effect, and that an actor need do no more than speak it clearly for it to have such an effect. We may feel more doubtful about the kinds of effect that actors of Hamlet have sought on the word 'father'. It comes within a verse line:

> I'll call thee Hamlet,
> King, father, royal Dane....

That Shakespeare has not given the word a climactic position may cause us to wonder whether he intended it to receive the emphasis that actors have given it. The effect can be judged only within the overall context of a particular performance. There it might seem like an irrelevant intrusion on the situation, or a brilliant illumination of it. If it were the second, the credit would be largely the actor's, even though he was working from, and partly through, the words that Shakespeare gave him to speak.

In these cases the actor at least has words to speak, even if what he does with them goes far beyond a straightforward expression of their immediate significance. Occasionally the performers are invited to achieve wordless effects if they can. In *The Knack*, for example, Ann Jellicoe has the direction, 'TOLEN *now pursues the intention of teasing* NANCY *and making her uncomfortable. He succeeds. If possible achieve this without words. But if necessary insert line*: "TOLEN: *Bit short in the neck. Nice hair though.*" ' At other times a dramatist may invite his interpreters to employ expressively silent reactions to what is spoken. A notable example occurs in Shakespeare's *Richard III.* The hunchback Gloster is welcoming the young Princes to London, where they will be housed in the Tower. They have a conversation, light-hearted on the surface but with sinister undertones. The young Duke of York is cheeky to his uncle, and his elder brother apologizes for him:

Uncle, your grace knows how to bear with him.

This leads to a punning speech from York:

You mean to bear me, not to bear with me.
Uncle, my brother mocks both you and me;
Because that I am little, like an ape,
He thinks that you should bear me on your shoulders.

Richard of Gloster makes no verbal reaction at all. Editors generally pass the moment by without comment. Some actors, however, have seen it as an opportunity for histrionic display, and have made much of Richard's silent reaction, suggesting that the boy's prattle wounds Richard in his most vulnerable spot, making him violently conscious of his deformity. Olivier's film version strongly emphasized the moment, with sudden close-ups and a discordant clash in the background music. This was perhaps a post-Freudian interpretative point, yet Shakespeare was clearly conscious of the psychological effects of physical deformity, and the actor here must be allowed full freedom of interpretation, whether to do nothing, something, or everything in response to the young prince's taunt.

An example of a brilliant theatrical stroke that may be

credited entirely to the actor was provided by Sir Laurence Olivier in his performance as Coriolanus. Kenneth Tynan described it:

> At the close, faithful as ever to the characterization on which he has fixed, Olivier is roused to suicidal frenzy by Aufidius's gibe—'thou boy of tears'. *'Boy!'* shrieks the overmothered general, in an outburst of strangled fury, and leaps up a flight of precipitous steps to vent his rage. Arrived at the top, he relents and throws his sword away. After letting his voice fly high in the great, swingeing line about how he 'flutter'd your Volscians in *Cor-i-o-li*', he allows a dozen spears to impale him. He is poised, now, on a promontory some twelve feet above the stage, from which he topples forward, to be caught by the ankles so that he dangles, inverted, like the slaughtered Mussolini. A more shocking, less sentimental death I have not seen in the theatre; it is at once proud and ignominious, as befits the titanic fool who dies it.

Olivier's death-fall was indeed intensely thrilling. I remember the shocked admiration with which the first-night audience witnessed it. And it was almost wholly the actor's creation. In the First Folio, the only authoritative text of the play, we find:

All Consp. Kill, kill, kill, kill, kill him.

> *Draw both the Conspirators, and kils*
> *Martius, who falles, Auffidius stands*
> *on him.*

The viciousness of the conspirators, the intensity, almost hysteria, of their blood-lust is evident. So is the ignominy

with which they treat Coriolanus's corpse. It may be that
the word 'falles' gave Olivier his hint. It probably means
simply that he falls from his standing posture before
Auffidius stands on him. By making him fall from a considerable height, and by doing so in a feat of remarkable
athleticism, Olivier created a startling visual image of
Coriolanus's downfall, the more ironically effective in that
the raised part of the stage on which he was stabbed
was that on which he had made his first, arrogant entry,
and from which he had cursed the 'common cry of
curs'. When he fell from it with a strangulated cry, to be
caught by the ankles and held dangling while Auffidius
stabbed him in the belly before he was lowered to the
stage level, both the magnitude and the squalor of his fall
were epitomized. Olivier's theatricalism had its critics.
Glynne Wickham seems to be girding at it when he writes,
'it is easy to obliterate the tragic stature of Coriolanus in
a matter of seconds by allowing him to leap to his death
in the manner of a trapeze-artist for the sake of the gasp
of surprise in the auditorium' (*Shakespeare's Dramatic
Heritage*, p. 235). It will serve nevertheless as an example
of a great moment in a Shakespeare performance which
seems to have been the creation of the actor rather than
the playwright.

In *Coriolanus* Olivier was working with a great play to
begin with. The leading role is one that may be expected
to prove a vehicle for display, and an actor could give a
great performance in it without any such additional
inventiveness as Olivier showed. There are, however,
roles in poor plays which too can be magnificently sustained. A good actor can sometimes hold and move an
audience with inferior material as well as with great. The
theatrical art, that is, is not dependent on the literary. A
few words or sentences that are of little significance on

the printed page may nevertheless be a wholly adequate basis for great moments, or indeed great sustained passages, of drama. To give examples from our own time may seem a little invidious, in that a modern play may appeal to us for many reasons which have nothing to do with its quality as literature or, in the long view, as drama. It is possible, to stay with the same actor for a moment, that John Osborne's *The Entertainer*, in which Olivier gave another memorable performance, was essentially such an 'actor's play'. An example from the past is that notorious melodrama, *The Bells*. Henry Irving's performance in it established him as a great actor. Gordon Craig was only one of many who were profoundly impressed by it. He wrote a remarkably vivid description of a moment in the play which may well pass for nothing at all in the reading. The central character, Mathias, has on his conscience a murder committed fifteen years before the action begins. In the first scene he comes home to his family after a visit to a neighbouring town, and as he is unbuttoning his gaiters he takes part in a conversation about a mesmerist. The relevant part of the dialogue is as follows:

> *Hans*   Ah! the Brigadier Stenger was telling me about it the other day. He had seen the same thing at Saverne. This Parisian sends people to sleep, and when they are asleep he makes them tell him everything that weighs upon their consciences.

> *Mathias*   Exactly.

The actor of Mathias has precisely one word—'exactly'—with which to make his effect. This is Gordon Craig's description of how Irving did it:

> Irving was buckling his second shoe, seated, and leaning over it with his two long hands stretched down

over the buckles. We suddenly saw these fingers stop
their work; the crown of the head suddenly seemed
to glitter and become frozen—and then, at the pace
of the slowest and most terrified snail, the two hands,
still motionless and dead, were seen to be coming
up the side of the leg ... the whole torso of the man,
also seeming frozen, was gradually, and by an almost
imperceptible movement, seen to be drawing up and
back, as it would straighten a little, and to lean a
little against the back of the chair on which he was
seated.

And then he whispered 'exactly'. Irving, it would appear,
thus created by purely physical, visual means an effect of
the revelation of a deeply disturbed conscience roughly
comparable to the poetic impact of one of Macbeth's
soliloquies, and did it without speaking a word.

What Craig describes is acting that is not dependent
upon words—acting between the lines, as it were. According to Henry James, it was because the play called for
this kind of acting that Irving was so successful in it—
'The more there is to act, and the less there is simply
to declaim, the better for Mr Irving, who owes his great
success in *The Bells* to the fact that the part of the dis-
tracted burgomaster is so largely pantomimic.' (*The Scenic
Art*, 1949, pp. 141-2.) The passage on which Craig comments is one in which the actor created an effect not
apparently envisaged by the author. That the author did
in general expect a great deal from his performers may
be gauged from the play's closing episode:

Mathias appears from the alcove—he is dressed in
the same clothes as when he retired into the alcove at
the commencement of the scene, but his face is

haggard, and ghastly pale—he comes out, his eyes
fixed, his arms extended—as he rushes forward with
uncertain steps, the crowd fall back with horror, and
form groups of consternation, with a general
exclamation of terror.

Mathias (in a voice of strangulation). The rope!
the rope! Cut the rope! (He falls suddenly, and is
caught in the arms of *Hans* and *Walter*, who carry
him to the chair in centre of stage. The Bells heard
off. Music, the melody played in the Second Act
when promise given. His hands clutch at his throat
as if to remove something that strangles him—he
looks pitifully round as if trying to recognize
those about him, and then his head falls on his breast.
Catherine, kneeling, places her hand on *Mathias's*
heart.)

Catherine   Dead! (The bells cease).

Annette bursts into tears. The *Women* in the crowd
kneel, the *Men* remove their hats and bend their heads
upon their breasts—tableau.

And the curtain falls. In this passage the writer is almost
as dependent on his actor as is the writer of a scenario for
an entirely wordless mime. The stage directions convey far
more than the dialogue. Indeed, a novelistic account of the
episode could be created from them with little alteration.
So far as the stage is concerned, the author has provided a
setting and a few properties; otherwise everything must
come from the actor playing Mathias. When that actor
was Irving, the play was brilliantly successful. No one else
has been able to make a comparable effect.

To say this is not to condemn *The Bells*. When we have
said that with Irving as Mathias it was successful we have
acknowledged that the writer is only one of the team

that is necessary to make a good play. We have admitted that Leopold Lewis wrote a script that, with a genius in the main role, provided an absorbing theatrical experience. We have not suggested that what he wrote has any literary value, or that it should have any intrinsic interest for later generations. It happened that Irving came upon a script that suited his talents peculiarly well; and the result has passed into theatrical history.

Perhaps the most extreme instances of great theatre having no dependence upon literary achievements are to be found in the music-hall and the related art of the silent film. Here again a script that has no value in itself may be transformed by the genius of the performer into a temporarily rich and meaningful experience. In the play-lets and sketches of the great performers there may exist a quality realizable only in performance and indissolubly linked to the particular performer. Max Beerbohm gives us something of this when he writes about the music-hall artist, Dan Leno:

> Apart from his personality and his technique, Dan Leno was, as I have said, a sayer of richly grotesque things. He had also a keen insight into human nature. He knew thoroughly, outside and inside, the types that he impersonated. He was always 'in the character,' whatever it might be. And yet if you repeat to any one even the best things that he said, how disappointing is the result! How much they depended on the sayer and the way of saying! I have always thought that the speech over Yorick's skull would have been much more poignant if Hamlet had given Horatio some specific example of the way in which the jester had been wont to set the table on a roar. We ought to have seen Hamlet convulsed with

laughter over what he told, and Horatio politely trying to conjure up the ghost of a smile.

In fact, Beerbohm goes on with a description of one of Leno's sketches which illustrates how an attempt to capture the art of the theatre may result in a piece of literary art:

I think I myself shall ever remember Dan Leno more vividly and affectionately as the shoemaker than as anything else. The desperate hopefulness with which he adapted his manner to his different customers! One of his customers was a lady with her little boy. Dan Leno, skipping forward to meet her, with a peculiar skip invented specially for his performance, suddenly paused, stepped back several feet in one stride, eyeing the lady in wild amazement. He had never seen such a lovely child. *How* old, did the mother say? Three? He would have guessed seven at least—'except when I look at you, ma'am, and then I should say he was one at most.' Here Dan Leno bent down, one hand on each knee, and began to talk some unimaginable kind of baby-language.... A little pair of red boots with white buttons? Dan Leno skipped towards an imaginary shelf; but, in the middle of his skip, he paused, looked back, as though drawn by some irresistible attraction, and again began to talk to the child. As it turned out, he had no boots of the kind required. He plied the mother with other samples, suggested this and that, faintlier and faintlier, as he bowed her out. For a few moments he stood gazing after her, with blank disappointment, still bowing automatically. Then suddenly he burst out into a volley of deadly criticisms on the

child's personal appearance, ceasing as suddenly
at the entrance of another customer.

Beerbohm continues in self-deprecatory fashion, regret-
ting that he has not been able more successfully to re-create
the occasion. Yet he has brilliantly described the kind of
sketch that succeeds only when performed by the actor
for whom it was created. Often enough such a sketch is
the work of the performer himself, or of someone so
closely associated with him that he knows how to provide an opportunity for the performer to do all the things
he does best. The monologues of Ruth Draper, the sketches
of comedians such as Al Read and Ken Dodd, offer other
examples. That their scripts would fall flat if performed
by anyone else is no criticism of them. The script is the
catalyst. It may be worthless as literature, offering nothing
to the reader, yet nevertheless be a good script in that it
enables the performer to give, perhaps, an impression of
richly individual character, or to convey a strong
emotional state. A parallel might be the way in which
some great songs have been composed to comparatively
trivial lyrics, or, perhaps more precisely, the way in which
a great musical interpreter can confer temporary distinction upon an inferior piece of music.

The inventive producer

The contribution of the individual performer, then, is
important; but a good production of a play is more than
the sum of the individual performances. A play works in
both time and space. Effects may be achieved by the
relative placing of actors on the stage, by the use of
repeated groupings or gestures, or by the kind of variety
within similarity which would illumine a point that

Granville-Barker made about the last scene of *King Lear*. Reminding us that the story of King Lear and Cordelia 'began for us with Lear on his throne, conscious of all eyes on him while she shamed and angered him by her silence', he points out in his 'Preface' to the play that in the last scene:

> The same company are here, or all but the same,
> and they await his pleasure. Even Regan and
> Goneril are here to pay him a ghastly homage.
> But he knows none of them—save for a blurred
> moment Kent whom he banished—none but
> Cordelia. And again he reproaches her silence; for
>   Her voice was ever soft,
>   Gentle and low, an excellent thing in woman.
> Then his heart breaks.

A producer might well care to recall the patterning of the opening scene at the play's ending. Some effects such as this may be seen to be built into the play, as if the author were thinking while he wrote in terms of the constantly changing stage picture. John Russell Brown describes Shakespeare's plays as scripts in which 'poetry, ambiguities, moral concepts and characterizations are inextricably involved with visual and temporal effects—compositions in form, colour and rhythm, devices of scale, contrast, repetition, sequence, tension and tempo.' In studying individual plays he tries, as he says, to show us 'the power of the "large and sweeping impression" of setting and movement, and to indicate what stage effects are required by the dialogue in addition to those described in the brief and often unreliable stage-directions.' And here he obliquely alludes to another of the areas of uncertainty that face us in the interpretation, not only of a Shakespeare play, but of any play for which we do not

have the author's detailed instructions as to stage movements, or the tradition of productions approved by the
author such as Stanislavski's of Chekov's plays. The work
of a critic who is skilled in the arts of the theatre as well
as literary criticism may draw our attention to some
examples of this kind of effect that may be supposed to
have occurred to Shakespeare. But an area of uncertainty
is bound to remain. Other effects, not implied by the text,
may have been intended though not transmitted to us.
And a producer is liable to create effects that are not true
to the author's concept: they may reinforce the true
intention of the play, they may add to it other, appropriate implications, or they may run counter to the play's
true direction. The achievements of the creative actor
may be matched by those of the inventive producer.

It is likely, of course, that Shakespeare himself was such
an inventive producer, and that as he composed he had
in mind the kind of instruction that he would give his
actors. The result may be a degree of deliberate—or at
least conscious—under-writing in parts of the plays. We
may feel that Shakespeare occasionally leaves too much
to his actors. In some scenes news of calamity can result
in an apparent banality of response that compels actors
to desperate efforts in the attempt to convey depths of
emotion through words that seem inadequate—as in
Hamlet, for instance, when Laertes responds to Gertrude's
information that his sister is drowned with the words
'Drowned! O, where?'; or in *Macbeth*, when Malcolm,
told 'Your royal father's murdered', responds with 'O, by
whom?' These are cases in which the actors seem to
require information as to the tone of voice they should
use, the emotions they are expected to convey. A case
might be made for the suggestion that Shakespeare is
portraying delayed shock, and that emotional numbness,

an anguished absence of comprehension, is the proper
impression to be conveyed. He himself shows awareness
of such a state of mind in *Richard II* (I. iv. 14-15), where
Aumerle says that he feigned

>   oppression of such grief
> That words seemed buried in my sorrow's grave.

There are other moments at which the action is in
doubt. The death of Coriolanus is an example; and there
are many other climactic points in the plays at which
by skilful grouping and timing a producer is almost certain to seek to create an intensity of effect which is not
apparent from the printed page. *All's Well that Ends Well*
affords a notable example in the final meeting of Helena
and Bertram, an effect that has its counterpart in *Measure
for Measure*, where Isabella kneels on behalf of Angelo.
It is not that the kneeling has to be imported into the
text, but that in order for this action to achieve its potential status of a moment of revelation it has to be built up
by theatrical means which in different productions are
likely to be variable, though their aims are comparable.
Moreover, if the producer and his actors are not sufficiently aware of the possibilities, the effect of what is
perhaps the most important moment of the play will be
less than it should be and, we may feel, the playwright's
achievement will be obscured.

Comic scenes, too, often depend upon an inventiveness
that is demanded by the text. It may be that while Shakespeare wrote, for example, the scene of midnight revelry
in *Twelfth Night*, involving Sir Toby, Sir Andrew, Feste,
Maria, and Malvolio, he had a clear notion of what he
wanted his actors to do. But he did not write it down, and
the result is that though the entry of Malvolio upon the
merrymaking obviously demands to be a great comic

moment, the precise means by which it is made so in the theatre is variable. It is comparable with the more sombre entry of the messenger of death into the hilarity of the last scene of *Love's Labour's Lost*, or the moment in *The Taming of the Shrew* when, after Bianca and the Widow to have sent their refusals to obey their husbands' requests, Katharina appears, finally tamed. This last is a moment to which one looks forward in any production of the play, not because one wonders whether Katharina will come or not, but because it is possible for a producer each time to create a sense of the miraculous, to make us share both the incredulity of those characters who believe, as Hortensio says, that 'she will not come', and also the emotions—not perhaps entirely confident—of Petruchio as he waits and is finally rewarded. It was especially moving in a Stratford production in which Peter O'Toole played Petruchio, giving a sense, as he strummed a lute and sang a strain of a song, that for him a great deal more than a hundred crowns hung upon the successful outcome of the wager; and in which Peggy Ashcroft, as Katharina, made a radiantly beautiful moment of her entry to make a public avowal of her transfiguration. In all these cases it would have been possible for Shakespeare to write stage directions plotting moves and business in great detail. He must have intended some elaboration of what he wrote. But he left no record of the details he envisaged, and modern producers are compelled either to rely on inauthentic tradition or to employ new methods of their own devising. We may never, then, see the play as its author planned it. And there are cases when we can say for certain that the author himself did not know exactly how his play should be performed. In his essay 'Poetry and Drama' T. S. Eliot has written amusingly of the appearance of the Furies in his play *The Family Reunion*

in a passage which demonstrates a playwright's readiness
to countenance variety of interpretation:

> I should either have stuck closer to Aeschylus or
> else taken a great deal more liberty with his myth.
> One evidence of this is the appearance of those
> ill-fated figures, the Furies. They must, in future,
> be omitted from the cast, and be understood to be
> visible only to certain of my characters, and not
> to the audience. We tried every possible manner
> of presenting them. We put them on the stage,
> and they looked like uninvited guests who had
> strayed in from a fancy-dress ball. We concealed
> them behind gauze, and they suggested a still
> out of a Walt Disney film. We made them dimmer,
> and they looked like shrubbery just outside the
> window. I have seen other expedients tried:
> I have seen them signalling from across the garden,
> or swarming on to the stage like a football team,
> and they are never right. They never succeed in
> being either Greek goddesses or modern spooks.

The nature of theatrical experience

A play has no constant theatrical reality. We cannot
subject ourselves to it as, for instance, succeeding generations have been able to subject themselves to the Sistine
Chapel, *Tom Jones*, or *City Lights* (for the film presumably
is the only art form dependent on time which remains
constant). There is a sense, then, in which *Hamlet* does
not exist. The words on the page are, we acknowledge,
not enough, even setting aside the fact that they are
themselves inconstant. And in the theatre we can never
see Shakespeare's *Hamlet*. We can see only a succession

of approximations to it, each of them nearer to or further from some kind of ideal performance, varying from one person to another, and likely to be modified each time we hear or see the play. We cannot even be sure that Shakespeare himself would have countenanced the notion of an ideal performance.

Having thus argued away the independent existence of all the world's greatest dramas, perhaps we should retreat a little and admit that, however variable the experiences that have been, are, and will be presented to us under the name of, for instance, *Hamlet*, they fall into two kinds: one that can be had from the reading of words on a page, the other from hearing these words, or words to the same effect, spoken with appropriate actions and movements in a theatre. And as sophistication sets in, the experiences are likely to mingle. When we see a play that we have read, we are likely to measure the performance against the impression formed from the printed page; and when we read a play that we have seen, our reading will be coloured by our memories of the performance, and we shall be obliged to acknowledge that, however intangible, the potential theatrical effect of a play is part of its significance.

2

The printing of plays

Dramatists and their interpreters

It is the inescapable fate of the dramatist that he can never
have complete control over what his work communicates.
He is, to put the matter at its simplest, at the mercy of
his interpreters. A writer who resents this, who knows
exactly what he wants to say, is likely, if he uses dramatic
forms at all, to write plays for reading only. But a writer
can respond to the possibility that his work will grow
once it has left his hands, that its potential meaning is
not limited as he is limited, but may profitably expand
even in ways that he has not foreseen. A playwright who
accepts this is liable to be less dogmatic about the way
his work should be performed than one who resents it.
Partly it is a matter of personality. Assertive writers, such
as Ben Jonson and George Bernard Shaw, have done all
in their power to ensure that their plays are presented
as they conceived them. Others have been more willing
to cut the umbilical cord. Many playwrights, whether
assertive or not, like to assist in the production of their
plays, and we know that they themselves frequently
make alterations during rehearsals. This may be the final,
perhaps unforeseen, stage in the process of composition.

Occasionally a play is published before it is performed, and a later edition will bear witness to the effect of theatrical performance. In *The Cocktail Party* (1949), for instance, T. S. Eliot acknowledges the help of the producer, E. Martin Browne, 'for suggestions most of which have been accepted, and which, when accepted, have all been fully justified on the stage'. Such alterations affected the printed text; the edition of 1950 bears the note 'certain alterations in Act III, based on the experience of the play's production, were made in the fourth impression of the text'.

But if a play has any success the author rapidly has to relinquish control. The script leaves his hands, is committed to print, and lives its own life. Many of its interpreters will wish simply to copy, so far as they can, a successful first production. But others will approach the script with a greater attempt to rethink the presentation and to shape the production to a different group of actors, even though this means diverging from the author's expressed intentions.

There are few expedients by which an author can guide interpretations over which he has no direct control, though he can do something by the manner in which he prepares the play for printing. He can write prefaces or notes, and he can use ample stage directions. One of the aims of this chapter will be to study the early history of the printing of plays, since the early period saw the establishment of conventions which (with certain modifications mentioned at the end of the chapter) have remained unchanged to the present day. The extent to which the presentation of plays in print is still governed by tradition is surprising. Many playwrights show little appreciation of the opportunities afforded by printing of presenting their plays either in a form suitable for reading, or in a manner that will make it easy for producers to deduce the author's intentions. We may be helped to understand why this should be so by glancing at the process by which plays are transmitted from their authors to their interpreters, and at the manner in which over the centuries plays have been presented on the printed page.

Limitations of the printed script

The words to be spoken in a play are generally conveyed from author to performers in writing, whether through manuscript, typescript, or print. A process of written transmission is likely to occur even when the author is himself closely associated with the performance, simply because it is the most convenient way for him to communicate to the actors what he wants them to say. An alternative would be for him to speak their lines to them and get them to memorize them thus. The suggestion seems ridiculous. We can imagine it happening only with children or in an experimental, semi-improvised work such as Peter Brook's *US*. But the fact that the written language is the normal medium between author and performers is crucial. There is one important theatrical art-form for which no satisfactory language exists, which is orally transmitted, and which has therefore preserved its theatrical purity. This is ballet. No one would think of studying ballet only by listening to the music written for it. We know that to experience it we need the visual as well as the aural medium, and as a result we are not subject to the temptations that the drama offers of substituting one kind of experience for another. But because the words of plays make some kind of sense even on the printed page, and because the language in which they are written is, unlike (for instance) musical notation, readily understandable, it is easy to assume that the reading of a play script is an adequate substitute for watching a performance. It is an accident that the instructions a playwright gives to his interpreters happen to provide something that is more or less able to stand on its own. Hence the form in which plays have usually been transmitted. But the script of a play rarely offers the reader much help to envisage the experience originally arrived at. The stage directions in most printed plays are inadequate if we think of them as intended to convey an impression of what happens on the stage over and above the speaking of words. This is because it is still customary to print plays from the script as written by the author, giving only a minimum of essential directions for entrances, exits, movements, and stage actions. Even in the theatre this has to be considerably amplified. The prompt book prepared primarily for the convenience of the stage-manager is generally a much fuller document, and often provides invaluable material for the stage-historian, but it is not readily accessible to the ordinary reader as it employs many abbreviations and technical terms.

It is, moreover, remarkable how many meaningless conventions are still often followed in the printing of plays. A standard modern edition of *Othello*, for example, gives us characters called Rod. (for Roderigo), Cas. (for Cassio), Bra. (for Brabantio), Sec. Sen. (for Second Senator), Mess. (for Messenger), and Des. (for Desdemona). This kind of mystification is a result of the lazy-minded acceptance of an ancient printing device presumably designed merely to save space, but perhaps resulting, too, from the blind copying by a compositor of abbreviations natural enough in an author's manuscript. Its survival in Shakespeare is

helped by the fact that a lengthy speech-prefix followed
by a blank verse line is apt to be too long to be fitted into
the width of the average-sized page, though there is no
reason why the name should not be printed above the
speech, as is done in some editions. Abbreviations are not
a serious obstacle to the sophisticated reader, who may
have read *Othello* many times and hardly needs to be
reminded who speaks what; but they are an unnecessary
hindrance to others, as well as a barbarism that would
not be countenanced in the printing of a novel:

> The R. Qu. broke the silence by saying to the
> Wh. Qu., 'I invite you to Al.'s dinner-party
> this afternoon.'
> The Wh. Qu. smiled feebly and said, 'And I
> invite *you*.'
> 'I didn't know I was to have a party at all,' said Al.,
> 'but if there is to be one, I think *I* ought to
> invite the guests.'

The preservation of such conventions may, however,
reflect an acknowledgement that a play is not intended
for reading, and by putting obstacles in the reader's way
may even have the salutary effect of forcing him to think
of the script as essentially incomplete. Still, at all times
the number of people interested in plays being produced
has been larger than the number who were able to see
them in production, if only for geographical reasons, and
so the reading of the scripts, however inadequately
presented, has been a necessary if an unnatural substitute,
and has been acknowledged as such from the time printing
was invented.

The first printed plays

The earliest printing of any English play that we have
dates from about 1512-16. The play, *Fulgens and Lucres*,
was written about 1495 by Henry Medwall, and is also
the first English secular drama to have survived. In one
respect at least it foreshadows a long tradition in the
printing of plays: nothing is done to assist the reader in
the absence of visual and aural effects. The few stage
directions are absolutely basic, and many important stage
happenings are not mentioned at all in the directions,
but have to be deduced from the dialogue. No editorial
process appears to have taken place. We are, of course,
short of evidence; but it seems reasonable to assume that
the script as prepared by the author for acting was simply
handed over for printing as it stood. We can say for certain, at least of the edition that has survived, that it was
not overseen by the author, as he had died some fifteen
years before.

The pattern adumbrated here has remained typical,
though by looking at the early history of the printing
of plays in England it is possible to make some deductions
about the readership of plays that publishers assumed,
and also to discern the emergence of a realization that
the printing process offered opportunities somewhat
different from those offered by the theatre.

For purposes of theatrical history the sixteenth century
divides into two eras, the first and longer being that of
the 'Tudor' plays, and the second seeing the beginnings
of 'Elizabethan' drama, with such dramatists as Peele,
Lyly, Greene, and Marlowe. We may take as a rough
dividing line the building in 1576 of the first English play-
house, called 'The Theatre', in Shoreditch. During the
earlier period a steady flow of plays came from the presses,

though by no means all have survived. Some editions have a distinctly practical look, and give information designed to help those who wish to perform the plays. Most professional acting companies of the time were small, and the doubling, trebling, or even quadrupling of parts was common. Before a group of actors could plan to put on a play they had to know that it was within their resources. Just as nowadays a catalogue of acting editions of plays is likely to include statements such as '5m. 3f.', so then many title pages bore assurances such as 'Six persons may easily play it' (*King Darius*) or 'Four may easily play this interlude' (*The Life and Repentance of Mary Magdalene*, by Lewis Wager). Some go into more detail. An example is the play called *The Conflict of Conscience*, printed in 1581 but written probably a good deal earlier. The title page of the printed text gives a list of the actors' names 'divided into six parts, most convenient for such as be disposed either to show this comedy in private houses, or otherwise'. We have, for example, 'Prologue, Mathetes, Conscience, Paphinitius for one', 'Satan, Tyrannye, Spirit, Horror, Eusebius for one', 'Avarice, Suggestion, Gisbertus, Nuntius for one', and so on. Only one role—that of Philologus—requires the attention of one actor throughout. There seems an effort on this title page to appeal to amateur as well as professional actors in the statement that the comedy may be shown 'in private houses or otherwise' (though of course at that time professionals might perform in private houses).

This presentation seems designed to appeal to potential performers rather than readers, and at least one 'Tudor' play, John Bale's *King John*, offers more assistance to performers by including unusually helpful stage directions which indicate the number of parts which actors were expected to undertake. We have, for instance, 'Go out England and dress for Clergy'; 'Here go out Usurped Power and Private Wealth and Sedition; Usurped Power shall dress for the Pope, Private Wealth for a Cardinal, and Sedition for a Monk ...' and so on. *King John* survives only in manuscript. If it had been printed, these instructions to its first performers would probably have been reproduced as they were written, with no intention of making the play more easily intelligible to those who simply read it. That such help is desirable may be deduced from the history of the criticism of this kind of play. It is a kind which is slowly coming to be understood, and at least partially rehabilitated, as the result of studies, such as David M. Bevington's *From 'Mankind' to Marlowe* (1962), which show us how to read early plays by providing the sort of information about their early performances which was taken for granted by authors and printers to such an extent that it was not thought worth mentioning in the printing.

Probably the cost of printing these plays could not have been justified if they had been intended only for potential performers. That there was a reading public as well is also suggested by some statements on the title pages. For instance, *The Life and Repentance of Mary Magdalene* (1566), by Lewis Wager, is 'not only godly, learned, and fruitful, but also well furnished with pleasant mirth and pastime, very delectable for those which shall hear or read the same'. *The Contract of a Marriage between Wit and Wisdom*, similarly, is 'very fruitful and mixed full of pleasant mirth as well for the beholders as the readers or hearers'. Many title pages of early plays stress their didactic, moralistic strain.

Authors and publishers of most secular literature at this time felt the need to claim morally-therapeutic virtues for their products. Every trivial romance of the period bears testimony to its morally restorative properties. But printers of plays may have made a special effort to appeal not so much to the world of popular entertainment (which in any case hardly existed) as to the narrowly constricted world of school plays, so schools may already have been thought of as a potential market.

For and against publication

We have unfortunately little positive evidence about the attitude of authors to the publication of their plays in this period; but the fairly general absence of prefatory material—dedications, epistles, and so on—suggests that they did not take their plays very seriously as literary products. But as the 'Tudor' period gives way to the 'Elizabethan' a new attitude begins to appear, and there are signs that writers wish their plays to be regarded as literary achievements.

The earliest plays to be printed with prefatory material are academic ones. The first of all seems to be Jasper Heywood's translation of Seneca's *Thyestes*, in 1560. The next, about ten years later, is the second edition of that most notorious of academic dramas, also associated with the Inns of Court, *Gorboduc*, by Sackville and Norton. John Day, the printer, has an epistle from 'The Printer to the Reader' which includes a statement that it was 'never intended by the authors thereof to be published'. This kind of disclaimer, however, is common enough in purely literary works, and especially understandable in that *Gorboduc* was written by aristocrats who would wish to dissociate themselves from any appearance of professionalism.

In 1578 comes one of the most interesting prefaces, George Whetstone's dedication to his massive two-part play *Promos and Cassandra*. Though this appears from the stage-directions to have been intended for performance, four years after its publication Whetstone wrote that it was 'yet never presented upon stage'. Probably he had failed to persuade anyone to act it, and therefore seized the opportunity to put it into print. Wounded vanity may partly account for his attack on the popular theatre of his time. The English playwright, he says, 'is most vain, indiscreet, and out of order. He first grounds his work on impossibilities, then in three hours runs he through the world, marries, gets children, makes children men, men to conquer kingdoms, murder monsters, and bringeth gods from heaven and fetcheth devils from hell.' He goes on to give his own prescription for a good play, laying particular stress on the moral. His own play, he claims, shows 'the confusion of vice and the cherishing of virtue'. ('The good ended happily', says Miss Prism, 'and the bad unhappily. That is what Fiction means.')

Whetstone's play, then, suggests publication as a disappointed playwright's substitute for performance. In 1576 was printed a piece which suggests strongly that a successful entertainment was likely to create a demand for a permanent souvenir in printed form. This is especially understandable since the entertainment was essentially unrepeatable, inseparable from the occasion for which it was conceived.

The Princely Pleasures at the Court at Kenilworth has an epistle by the printer in which he says he has heard that in the Queen's last progress she was 'honourably and triumphantly received and entertained' by the Earl of Leicester at Kenilworth, 'and that sundry pleasant and poetical inventions were there expressed, as well in verse as in prose. All which have been sundry times demanded for as well at my hands as also of other printers, for that indeed all studious and well-disposed young gentlemen and others were desirous to be partakers of those pleasures by a profitable publication.' He explains that he has gone to great trouble to obtain 'the very true and perfect copies' not only of the pieces that were performed, but also of one which 'never came to execution'. Obviously this was a newsworthy occasion, and a unique one, not precisely comparable with the public performance of a play which might be repeated as often as there was a demand for it. The printer hoped and expected by supplying the demand to find this a 'profitable publication' in the financial sense.

It is not till the 1590s that the inclusion of prefatory material with the printed text of a play performed in the public theatres becomes at all common. In 1590 Marlowe's *Tamburlaine* was printed with a preface again by the printer, not the author. The printer was Richard Jones, who had also been responsible for both *Promos and Cassandra* and *The Princely Pleasures*—obviously he liked acting as presenter to his own entertainments. The epistle to *Tamburlaine* is especially interesting in that it indicates editorial intervention designed to improve the play for reading. Jones, addressing 'the gentlemen readers and others that take pleasure in reading histories', expresses his hope that the two 'tragical discourses' of *Tamburlaine* 'will be now no less acceptable unto you to read after your serious affairs and studies than they have been lately delightful for many of you to see when the same were showed in London upon stages'. He seems, that is, to be hoping for a readership composed partly of those who have not seen the plays, and partly of those who have. The reading is expected to provide entertainment—'after your serious affairs and studies'—but nevertheless the printer claims to have removed some of the lighter matter. 'I have purposely omitted and left out some fond and frivolous gestures, digressing, and in my poor opinion, far unmeet for the matter.' These comic episodes, he continues, have been popular on the stage, but 'now to be mixtured in print with such matter of worth, it would prove a great disgrace to so honourable and stately a history'. Thus early do we find an expression of the essentially snobbish point of view that the printing of a dramatic work confers upon it a dignity that it must have lacked in performance. On the other hand, the implied distinction between matter which is suitable for reading, and that which is appropriate only to perform-ance, is realistic enough.

Jones refers in the epistle to those who have seen the plays 'showed in London upon stages'. Those who lived in London, or frequently visited it, could of course go to the theatres and see plays again and again if they wished, for as long as the plays remained in a company's reper-tory. And as long as a play retained theatrical drawing power it was in the interests of the company not to print it—or at any rate this seems to have been the companies' attitude. Probably the fear was not so much that people would read the play instead of going to see it, as that once it had appeared in print it would be available for the use of other, rival companies of actors. In 1600, for instance, the Admiral's Men borrowed forty shillings 'to give unto the printer to stay the printing of *Patient Grissell*', and in 1608 a group of London companies made a formal agreement that they would not allow the publi-cation of their play-books. Surreptitious copies of plays sometimes appeared, resulting in that class of texts which we have come to call 'bad quartos'. The most notable instance is Shakespeare's *Hamlet*, and perhaps the most surprising thing about the quarto that appeared in 1603 is that anybody bothered to print it at all. The printers must have been trying to cash in on a major theatrical success; but if the play was ever acted or read in the shape in which it was first printed it must have caused serious disappointment. A good version appeared soon afterwards. For once a company permitted a play to appear while it was still 'good box-office' in order to correct a false impression that might have been conveyed by the wretchedness of the first printed text. There are other cases, too, in which the text of a printed play is so bad that its being offered for either reading or acting can be regarded only as a confidence trick.

But there must have been a good market for plays, for they were printed in large numbers even after they had lost their first novelty. To whom did they appeal? We lack information about the Elizabethan reading public. We know that the Queen's godson, Sir John Harington, had in his library 129 plays. He seems to have accumulated them over a period of about ten years—E. K. Chambers computes that he possessed 90 out of the 105 plays printed during that period. Clearly he was an acquisitive collector, but we have no means of knowing whether he had any special reason for wanting plays.

A collector who had such a reason was Sir Edward Dering, of Surrenden in Kent, who is known to have put on amateur performances, including one of Shakespeare's *Henry IV*. His account-books reveal that he was a keen theatre-goer. Between 1619 and 1626, for instance, he saw twenty-seven plays, all in London except for one in Maidstone. His theatre visits were more frequent after his wife died, in 1622, than they had been before then. And during a shorter period—1619 to 1624—he bought at least 221 books of plays, sometimes in lots of twenty or thirty at once. Unfortunately we know the titles of only a few of them. Sometimes he bought several copies of a single play; and on December 5, 1623, he entered:

2 volumes of Shakespear's playes 02. 00 00
Johnson's plays 00. 09 00

He had some of his plays bound up. About 1625 his interest in the theatre began to give way to antiquarian pursuits. Dering's interest seems to have been partly that of the amateur actor, and we have no evidence that he regarded the texts he bought as 'literature'.

Doubtless others, too, bought plays as possible acting texts. It would be interesting to know what circulation plays had in the provinces. Did the culturally deprived dweller in provincial towns and villages buy texts of plays that were successful in London, while dreaming of the next visit to his neighbourhood of a touring troupe of actors? Were plays bought largely as souvenirs by those who had already seen them acted? Were they bought by readers and enjoyed as reading matter, as tales or poems which happened to be in dramatic form? This last would seem a reasonable enough possibility, especially considering the generally low standard of prose fiction at the time. Yet if it had been so we might have expected more signs of it in the manner in which plays were printed. With few exceptions, plays of the popular theatres continued to be printed with little care; without, it would seem, the superintendence of their authors, without the panoply of epistles, dedications, and commendatory verses that frequently accompanied more self-consciously literary works, most of which are now far less regarded than many of the plays of the time. The example of Shakespeare is the best known. He was an unusually successful dramatist, in print as well as on the stage. *Richard II* appeared in six editions from 1597 to 1623; *Henry IV, Part One* in seven editions from 1598 to 1623; *Romeo and Juliet* five times from 1597 to 1623. And these were commercial editions, intended to make money. Yet in not one of his plays published in his lifetime is there anything to dignify it as a work of literature—no dedication, no epistle, no commendatory poem. The only partial exception is *Troilus and Cressida*, the 1609 edition of which has a printer's epistle. What is more, about half of Shakespeare's plays were not printed till seven years after he died. We may contrast this with the situation in regard to his narrative poems. *Venus and Adonis*, carefully printed in 1593 with the author's own dedication to the Earl of Southampton, appeared in sixteen editions between then and 1640—eleven up to 1617; and *Lucrece*, which first appeared a year later than *Venus and Adonis*, also with a dedication to Southampton, went through six editions up to 1616. Here obviously was Shakespeare, the man of letters, making his bid for fame. So far as he was concerned, the theatre was its own medium, and the publication of the plays was little more important than, perhaps, the provision of a printed libretto at the performance of an opera.

For most playwrights, as for Shakespeare, we have only the negative evidence of what they did not do; but a few distinctly disclaimed the intention of being read. Thomas Heywood, for example, in an epistle to *The Rape of Lucrece* (1608), writes: 'It hath been no custom in me of all other men, courteous readers, to commit my plays to the press ... for though some have used a double sale of their labours, first to the stage, and after to the press, for my own part I here proclaim myself ever faithful in the first, and never guilty of the last.' There was a certain consistency in his attitude, for much later—in 1633—he wrote:

> True it is that my plays are not exposed unto the
> world in volumes to bear the title of *Works*—as
> others; one reason is that many of them by shifting
> and change of companies have been negligently lost,
> others of them are still retained in the hands of some
> actors, who think it against their peculiar profit to
> have them come in print, and a third, that it never
> was any great ambition in me to be in this kind
> voluminously read.

Heywood was an exceedingly prolific writer of plays (he
claimed that there were two hundred and twenty in which
'I have had either an entire hand, or at the least a main
finger'), and his statement that 'in this kind' he did not
care to be voluminously read is borne out by the fact
that many of his plays were never printed, and of those
that were, several were unauthorized issues—which shows
that they were nevertheless thought of as a reasonable
commercial speculation. He printed works in other kinds
as well. As Arthur Brown suggests in an article called
'The Printing of Books', (*Shakespeare Survey 17*, p. 205),
Heywood seems to have felt it was worth his while wholly
to commit himself to the interests of the actors and that
'there was nothing further to be gained by chasing after
the dubious immortality of print'.

Heywood's excuse for permitting some of his plays to
appear in print was that this at least gave him the opportunity of making sure that it was done properly. In a stage
prologue written for a revival of *If You Know Not Me, You
Know Nobody*, he 'taxeth the most corrupted copy now
imprinted, which was published without his consent', and
implies that it was so popular that 'some by stenography
drew | The plot, put it in print—scarce one word true.'
John Marston writes in similar, though more cantankerous,

vein in his epistle to *The Malcontent* (1604). His statement is particularly interesting because he not merely disclaims the apparent pretentiousness of permitting his play to reach print, but rather expresses his awareness that the reading of a work intended to be seen may misrepresent his achievement.

> Only one thing afflicts me, to think that scenes
> invented merely to be spoken, should be enforcively
> published to be read, and that the least hurt I can
> receive is to do myself the wrong. But since others
> otherwise would do me more, the least inconvenience
> is to be accepted. I have myself therefore set forth this
> comedy, but so that my enforced absence must much
> rely upon the printer's discretion. But I shall entreat
> slight errors in orthography may be as slightly
> o'erpassed, and that the unhandsome shape which
> this trifle in reading presents may be pardoned for
> the pleasure it once afforded you when it was
> presented with the soul of lively action.

Here is a hint that Marston recognized that the true life of a play is on the stage, that those will read it best who have already seen it performed, and that the printed text is a body without a soul.

Heywood's boast that his 'plays are not exposed unto the world in volumes to bear the title of *Works*—as others' is clearly a dig at the attitude of those authors who consciously made a bid for immortality on the strength of stage works. It is probable that the remark was aimed particularly at Ben Jonson.

Jonson's revolutionary stand

Jonson, if anyone, laboured to confer literary respectability upon the popular drama. He did so, paradoxically enough, partly out of dissatisfaction with it—or, at least, with those conditions prevailing in the popular theatre that made it difficult for him to do within the limits of the medium all that he would have liked to do. Early in his career he published plays with evident concern for their presentation as reading matter. Indeed the manner in which he presented the first of his writings to reach print may well suggest that its publication represented for him the kind of bid for literary recognition that, seven years previously, Shakespeare had made with *Venus and Adonis*. The touch of characteristic defiance in Jonson's case is that his work is a play. *Every Man out of his Humour* appeared in 1600, and with an important state-ment on its title page: '*The Comical Satire of Every Man Out of his Humour*. As it was first composed by the author B.I. Containing more than hath been publicly spoken or acted.' So far as I know, this is the first time we are told on a title page that the play as printed contains more than had been used in the theatre. The implication is that the play as written was too long for the actors. Similar statements are made later in connexion with other plays. Barnabe Barnes's *The Devil's Charter*, 1607, is said to be printed 'As it was played ... But more exactly reviewed, corrected, and augmented since by the author, for the more pleasure and profit of the reader'; and Webster's *The Duchess of Malfi*, in 1623, has 'divers things printed that the length of the play would not bear in the presentment'. But Jonson goes further than this with *Every Man out of his Humour*. Indeed he goes so far that it is difficult not to suspect that behind its printing lies a quarrel with the company that presented it. The dedication to the Inns of Court includes a conventional enough statement that 'the printer ... thinks it worthy a longer life than commonly the air of such things doth promise'. The printer himself contributes a somewhat enigmatic note, saying: 'It was not near his thoughts that hath published this, either to traduce the author or to make vulgar and cheap any the peculiar and sufficient deserts of the actors; but rather—whereas many censures fluttered about it—to give all leave, and leisure to judge with distinction.' What exactly all this means is not clear; but it is plain that there have been differences of opinion, and that publication of the play is ostensibly intended to give the opportunity for objective judgments to be formed.

Certainly this play is unusually carefully prepared for reading. There is, for example, what the title page calls 'the several character of every person'. Jonson gives, that is, not simply a list of *dramatis personae*, but a brief character sketch of each of them. There are many ways in which Jonson seems to anticipate Shaw, and this is one of them—though Shaw, of course, generally distributes his character sketches among the stage directions instead of prefacing the play with them. Jonson's have a strongly literary character. They are concise and pungent, all of them worth quoting, and some of them envisaging a kind of off-stage life for the characters of the play. Take Fastidious Brisk for example:

A neat, spruce, affecting courtier, one that wears clothes well, and in fashion; practiseth by his glass how to salute; speaks good remnants, notwithstanding the bass viol and tobacco; swears tersely, and with variety; cares not what lady's favour he belies, or great man's familiarity; a good property to perfume the boot of a coach. He will borrow another man's horse to praise, and backs him as his own. Or, for a need, on foot can post himself into credit with his

merchant only with the jingle of his spur and the
jerk of his wand.

This obviously is a self-conscious kind of literary exercise;
it is not surprising that Douglas Bush, in his Oxford History, *English Literature in the Earlier Seventeenth Century*,
classifies these character sketches among the earliest mani-
festations of the development of the English school of
character-writers.

Another interesting feature of this edition is the evidence
that it provides of theatrical changes made during the
course of production, and the author's resentment of them.
The play proper ends with an epilogue, and then on the
next page is the statement 'It had another *Catastrophe* or
Conclusion at the first playing: which ... many seemed
not to relish it; and therefore 'twas since altered; yet that
a right-eyed and solid reader may perceive it was not so
great a part of the heaven awry as they would make it, we
request him but to look down upon these following reasons'.
There follows an apology which reveals that originally
the play's dénouement had been brought about by the
appearance on stage of an actor impersonating the Queen,
an occurrence frowned upon at that time almost as much
as it would be today. And Jonson reprints part, at least, of
the original 'catastrophe'. The text of the play is prepared
with quite unusual care; and though the original stage
directions are not excessively ample, they are lavish
enough to suggest that Jonson may have been aware of the
needs of a reader. They include the kind of information
that often has to be editorially supplied for a Shakespeare
play—instructions for the characters to 'salute as they
meet in the walk', to go 'aside', to speak 'as they pass over
the stage', or to walk off 'meditating'. There is even a
series of instructions as to the precise points at which one

of the actors should take tobacco, provoking the response
'I ne'er knew tobacco taken as a parenthesis before'.

The fullness with which Jonson prepared *Every Man
out of his Humour* for reading may have been a result of
its topical interest as well as of his desire to enshrine his
play in an appropriate setting. That it had topical interest
is witnessed by the fact that it was printed three times in
1600, though not again till 1616. But once having started
on this course, Jonson continued on it. A prominent
instance is his classical tragedy *Sejanus*, clearly an
extremely 'literary' work, though one which was first
presented, unsuccessfully, on the stage. Jonson prints it
with a dedication in which he says: 'It is a poem that, if
I well remember, in your lordship's sight suffered no less
violence from our people here than the subject of it did
from the rage of the people of Rome.' He claims that
nevertheless it has outlived its audience's malice. In his
address 'To the Readers' he invites comparison between
his play and the dramatic laws of antiquity, claiming that
though he may not have followed all the forms, still 'in
truth of argument, dignity of persons, gravity and height
of elocution, fullness and frequency of sentence' he has
'discharged the other offices of a tragic writer'. He tells us
too once again 'that this book, in all numbers, is not the
same with that which was acted on the public stage;
wherein a second pen had good share'.

The dignity of the publication is further kept up by the
printing of commendatory verses by, among others, Chap-
man and Marston, and of an 'argument' or summary of the
plot. The play itself is remarkable for the liberality of
annotation with which Jonson has graced it. Literally
hundreds of notes give sources in classical literature, and
the notes are written in Latin. Jonson is treating his own
play as if it were a classical text. Even he seems to have

been a little embarrassed by it. In his epistle he says 'lest in some nice nostril the quotations might savour affected, I do let you know that I abhor nothing more; and have only done it to show my integrity in the story and save myself in those common torturers that bring all wit to the rack'. As he points out, the notes are in Latin, like most of the works to which they refer, so 'it was pre-supposed none but the learned would take the pains to confer them'.

Other quartos of Jonson's plays, too, were prepared with great care by the author. *Volpone* is a notable example; so is his other classical tragedy, *Catiline*, in which in a characteristically ungracious dedication he congratulates his dedicatee on daring, 'in these jig-given times, to countenance a legitimate poem'. It has a phenomenally insulting epistle 'To the Reader in Ordinary', and it is clear that Jonson is claiming a dissociation between himself and the popular drama. As in so much that he writes, we feel that he considered himself to be working on a dif-ferent level of endeavour from that of most of his con-temporaries, and one that has strong affinities with the classical dramatists. Many of his contemptuous comments on the popular drama of his time are well known; and we are likely to feel that he was too much inclined to suppose that the only way in which he could express a merit comparable to that which he discerned in the classical writers was by displaying a knowledge of, and even to some extent desiring to imitate, their work.

The climax of Jonson's campaign to demonstrate his literary respectability within the genre of stage pieces comes in 1616 with the publication of his *Works*. This was the grand gesture, and it represents a landmark in the history of the presentation of English plays as literature. No English writer for the popular stage had previously published his collected plays as his 'works', though some plays, mostly academic in nature, had appeared in collections of their author's writings. Jonson's is a handsome volume of more than a thousand pages, with an elaborately designed, emblematic title page bearing a defiant motto:

neque me ut miretur turba, laboro;
contentus paucis lectoribus

—the Latin is part of the defiance—'I don't work to be gaped at by the mob, but am happy with a few readers.' This, characteristically, is adapted from one of Horace's satires. There are commendatory verses, some of them reprinted from the quartos; and the plays are given along with information about the date, company, and actors in their first performances. Many of the texts are corrected, some of them extensively revised. The volume opens with the very thoroughly revised version of *Every Man in his Humour*, a revision in which the scene is laid in England instead of Italy, and which may have been made specifically for the 1616 Folio. Passages that had had to be omitted from plays for topical reasons when they were printed in quarto are restored, notably some Court satire in *Cynthia's Revels*.

Facts such as these make it clear that Jonson was himself closely concerned with the printing of this volume. The very layout of the plays is indicative both of the thought that went into it, and also of the link that Jonson was concerned to make between himself and the classical drama. As his editors say,

In contrast to the form in which other people's plays and his own earlier quartos were printed, he copied the setting of the old Greek and Latin comedians originally adopted in the first editions of Plautus

(Venice, Merula, 1472), Terence (Strassburg, Rusch, 1470), Aristophanes (Aldus, 1498). The speeches in dialogue are printed continuously, running on even lines. With these classical authors the system continues to this day.

The names of the speakers in a given scene are grouped at the beginning of it. In various other technical details the presentation is rethought with obvious care, often aimed at approximating more closely to the practice followed in editions of the classics. This extends to the spelling and the punctuation. The volume was much corrected while it passed through the press; Jonson himself probably worked regularly at the printing house for much of the period that the volume was being prepared.

Unfortunately we have no reviews to give us any indication of how his book was received; but there is no reason to suppose that it was a commercial failure. Some felt that Jonson had been pretentious, and had overreached himself. Two epigrams are preserved, of which the first was addressed:

> *To Mr Ben Jonson demanding the reason why he called his plays 'works'.*
> Pray tell me, Ben, where doth the mystery lurk:
> What others call a play you call a work.

The second is headed:

> *Thus answered by a friend in Mr Jonson's defence.*
> The author's friend thus for the author says,
> Ben's plays are works, when others' works are plays.

Heywood's comment of 1633 that 'my plays are not exposed unto the world in volumes to bear the title of

Works—as others' has already been quoted. Two years earlier he had written, 'my plays have not been exposed to the public view of the world in numerous sheets, and a large volume; but singly, as thou seest, with great modesty and small noise'. And Sir John Suckling wrote more good-humouredly:

> The first that broke silence was good old Ben,
> Prepared before with canary wine,
> And he told them plainly he deserved the bays,
> For his were called *Works*, where others' were but
> plays.

In spite of this mockery, Jonson's gesture succeeded. 'Not only', writes J. B. Bamborough, 'did his example cause a general rise in the standard of printing plays (and very likely gave Heminge and Condell the idea of collecting Shakespeare's works in folio); since his time nobody has seriously denied the right of plays to be considered as literature.'

The Shakespeare Folio

The next dramatist whose plays were published in folio was Shakespeare; and it is appropriate that the first words printed in the volume—the address 'To the Reader'—should be by Jonson. The title page, we cannot help remarking, does not describe these plays as 'Works'; they are 'Mr William Shakespeare's Comedies, Histories, and Tragedies, published according to the true original copies'. They are printed along with a portrait of the author (Jonson had not gone as far as that—but Shakespeare, after all, was dead), a dedication, another epistle, and a variety of commendatory verses, including Jonson's great tribute. The texts themselves, unfortunately, have not undergone as careful supervision as Jonson had devoted to his own plays, though Heminge and Condell, who were responsible for the volume, were not without editorial concerns and capacities. The Shakespeare Folio has a list of 'the names of the principal actors in all these plays', and it may be only because Shakespeare was so closely bound up with the affairs of a single company that we do not have the more detailed information about the plays' early performances provided by the Jonson Folio. There is much about Shakespeare's plays that we do not know and that we should be likely to know if they had been Jonson's. Yet Shakespeare would have been the less Shakespeare had he displayed the egotism and self-esteem that contributed to Jonson's concern for his own immortality. The Shakespeare Folio does not tell us all we should like to know, but it does one supremely important thing: it provides us with the texts of plays that had not previously been printed, and that might otherwise have been lost to us. Had it not been for Jonson's example and, we may conjecture, encouragement, Shakespeare might have been known today by only about half of his output, for the greatest of all collections of plays as literature might not have appeared.

Modern editors, and George Bernard Shaw

In essentials the manner of presenting plays in print has not changed much since the time of Jonson and Shakespeare. There have been developments, of course. Illustrated editions have become common, adorned sometimes with engravings or photographs of the plays in performance, sometimes with representations of the action as if it had really happened, sometimes with abstract or symbolic designs. Plays, ancient and modern, appear sometimes in editions specifically intended for performers, sometimes in ones aimed at particular groups of readers. These may include much annotation, along with introductions, appendices, and so on, but so far as the text is concerned it is still customary to print the words to be spoken along with only brief indications of the necessary action, accompanied perhaps in more laconic prose dramas with a few indications of the states of mind that the performers are supposed to convey.

Some writers, however, have discerned the commercial advantages in making their scripts as accessible as may be to a reading public. Allardyce Nicoll (in *English Drama: A Modern Viewpoint* (1968), pp. 108-9) refers to the invention at the end of the nineteenth century of

> stage-directions which went beyond the strict limits of the stage itself, providing a kind of narrative calculated to make the dialogue of interest even to those who had not had the opportunity of seeing the plays in action. Hitherto the literary and the theatrical had tended to remain distinct from each other, whereas during the last two decades of the nineteenth century they inclined to draw together, and consequently the basis for future endeavours was being surely laid.

There is an interesting discussion of this matter in Bernard Shaw's Preface to his *Plays Unpleasant*. 'The dramatic author', he says, 'has reasons for publishing his plays which would hold good even if English families went to the theatre as regularly as they take in the newspaper. A perfectly adequate and successful stage representation of a play requires a combination of circumstances so extraordinarily fortunate that I doubt whether it has ever occurred in the history of the world.' Here Shaw is

acknowledging the necessary gap between what the playwright asks of his performers and what they can give him,
and he implies that the existence of a reading text may do
something to correct false impressions received in the
theatre. He takes Shakespeare as an example, saying that
if he (Shaw) had not read the plays as well as seeing them,
his 'impression of them would be not merely incomplete,
but violently distorted and falsified'. To some extent this
is intended as an attack on the extreme freedom of adaptation customary in the presentation of Shakespeare's plays
in the late nineteenth- and early twentieth-century theatre,
but Shaw says too that while

> the living author can protect himself against this
> extremity of misrepresentation ... the more
> unquestioned is his authority on the stage, and the
> more friendly and willing the co-operation of the
> manager and the company, the more completely does
> he get convinced of the impossibility of achieving an
> authentic representation of his piece as well as an
> effective and successful one.... Not even when a
> drama is performed without omission or alteration
> by actors who are enthusiastic disciples of the author
> does it escape transfiguration.

And from this he goes on to state his conviction that the
reading of plays is a necessary complement to seeing them
performed. 'I have never found an acquaintance with a
dramatist founded on the theatre alone, or with a composer founded on the concert room alone, a really intimate
and accurate one. The very originality and genius of the
performers conflicts with the originality and genius of
the author.'
    Shaw is ready to acknowledge that the result of such

conflicts may make for exciting theatre, and he entertainingly imagines Shakespeare congratulating Henry Irving on a misrepresentation of Shylock which would be highly profitable to both author and actor. But the didactic Shaw, while happy that his plays should entertain, was also anxious that his ideas should be propagated, that his plays should mean what he intended them to mean. So he continues:

> the fact that a skilfully written play is infinitely more adaptable to all sorts of acting than available acting is to all sorts of plays (the actual conditions thus exactly reversing the desirable ones) finally drives the author to the conclusion that his own view of his work can only be conveyed by himself. And since he could not act the play singlehanded even if he were a trained actor, he must fall back on his powers of literary expression, as other poets and fictionists do.

Of course it might be fairer to say that the author who wishes to put forward his own point of view unmistakably should eschew the dramatic form: but Shaw (as usual) wants the best of all worlds—the freedom and allure offered by the theatre along with a personal expressiveness more appropriate to other literary forms. But at least he perceives that the printing of plays offers possibilities beyond the theatrical: 'So far,' he goes on, 'this has hardly been seriously attempted by dramatists. Of Shakespear's plays we have not even complete prompt copies: the folio gives us hardly anything but the bare lines. What would we not give for the copy of *Hamlet* used by Shakespear at rehearsal, with the original stage "business" scrawled by the prompter's pencil? And if we had in addition the descriptive directions which the author gave on the stage:

above all, the character sketches, however brief, by which he tried to convey to the actor the sort of person he meant him to incarnate'—the sort of thing, that is, that Jonson gives us in *Every Man out of his Humour*—'what a light they would shed, not only on the play, but on the history of the sixteenth century! Well, we should have had all this and much more if Shakespear, instead of merely writing out his lines, had prepared the plays for publication in competition with fiction as elaborate as that of Meredith.' Shaw goes on to claim that it is 'for want of this elaboration' that Shakespeare 'has left us no intellectually coherent drama'. This is a false conclusion. The intellectual coherence of a play, even by Shaw, is not necessarily to be found only in its prefaces or stage directions. Shaw is here trying to cast Shakespeare in his own mould. He falsifies too by exaggeration when he claims that modern plays need 'literary treatment' far more than Shakespeare's 'because in his time the acting of plays was very imperfectly differentiated from the declamation of verses'; indeed some of Shaw's plays require a style of acting still less imperfectly differentiated from the declamation of prose; but there is some justice in his generalization that modern plays, depending more than most Elizabethan ones on stage business, and being less expressive in their style, stand more in need of literary presentation. So Shaw is justly surprised that 'the presentation of plays through the literary medium has not yet become an art' and that therefore 'it is very difficult to induce the English public to buy and read plays'. He concludes that there is an overwhelming case 'not only for printing and publishing the dialogue of plays, but for a serious effort to convey their full content to the reader', and refers to his own 'bald attempts' which soon 'will be left far behind'. They have not been. Other playwrights have done something—Sir James Barrie, for instance. Some editors have done it for Shakespeare. The earlier volumes of the New Cambridge Shakespeare include some very 'literary' expansions of the original stage directions. In *A Midsummer Night's Dream*, for example, we find:

> *Another part of the wood. A grassy plot before a great oak-tree; behind the tree a high bank overhung with creepers, and at one side a thorn-bush. The air is heavy with the scent of blossom.* Titania *lies couched in her bower beneath the bank; her fairies attending her.*

This is awkwardly poised between the literary and the theatrical. 'The scent of blossom' is not something that we expect to experience in the theatre, and the representational particularity of setting that the direction implies belongs to the theatre of Barrie rather than Shakespeare. Directions such as these, in which literary modes are juxtaposed, may cause us to feel that something is lost when plays are given a 'literary treatment', at least unless it derives from their authors. And the fact that their authors have not usually seen fit to give them such treatment, even when (like Henry James) they had a great deal of experience of writing the description round the dialogue, may suggest a recognition that the successful dramatist must be willing not to 'tell all'; that the theatre has something to contribute, and that his play cannot fully spring to life by his own unaided efforts. When it does spring to life it may, like any offspring, surprise its parent.

3

The intent and the event

Characteristics of the masque

The previous chapter has been concerned mainly with the growth of early attitudes towards the printing of plays, with speculation about their readership, and with the fact that dramatists have been content with little development in methods of presenting plays for reading since the publication of the Shakespeare First Folio. A conclusion that might be drawn is that writers have felt justified in making demands upon their readers' imagination; that the wisest of them, at least, though they have been willing to allow their plays to be published, and have sometimes added passages that had been omitted in the theatre, have not tried to give their scripts full coherence as objects for reading. (It is, incidentally, interesting that the adaptation of novels into plays has been both more common and more successful than the reverse process.) The present chapter will turn to the examination of a particular instance of discrepancy between printed text and performance. The work chosen is a masque, *Pleasure Reconciled to Virtue*, by Ben Jonson. The masque genre is particularly relevant to the topic of this book because it presents an extreme case of a theatrical script in dramatic form which gives only a very limited, partial impression of the performance that it represents, but nevertheless has literary value. It belongs to those types of dramatic entertainment which their authors have been particularly anxious to see in print. These include works intended for a certain, unrepeatable occasion, and ones written in a highly-wrought, 'literary' style. I have mentioned the printing in 1576 of the script of an entertainment given before Queen Elizabeth at Kenilworth, and suggested that it was particularly understandable that such an entertainment, having strong topical interest, should be soon published so that those who were not privileged to be present could nevertheless share something of the excitement. There exist many descriptions during the Elizabethan period (and others) of such entertainments given before the royal family. Often they are purely spectacular, with no literary content at all. However, from them there gradually emerged the kind of dramatic spectacle known as the masque, in which the art of the playwright, or poet, had a considerable share, and of which the fruits of his art are, often enough, all that survive. The scripts (or libretti) of masques are often read as literature, and many of them are by writers whom we think of as poets rather than playwrights. The best known of all is Milton's *Comus*. One reason why it is so well known is that it is one of the least typical, for in its composition Milton was the dominant partner. It is more a work of pure literature than most other specimens of the kind, and so can more easily be read as a poem; though even it cannot be properly appreciated without consideration of the context for which it was created. Many other masques contain fine writing, and if they are not read as often as they might be, this is largely because, in spite of their literary qualities, they are more difficult to read properly than most plays.

The difficulty is one of imaginative effort. A masque was essentially a collaborative enterprise, the product of the combined talents of many different contributors. It required not only someone to write dialogue and words for songs, but also a designer of costumes and scenery and machinery, a composer, a dancing master or choreographer, actors, and dancers.

The same is true of many a play; but with a masque the balance tends to be different. The controlling mind of a play is the author's. His is the final responsibility. This was not necessarily true of a masque. The greatest of the masque writers was Ben Jonson, and it is hardly surprising that he, with his strong personality, should have found it difficult to subdue himself to the occasion and to work harmoniously with his collaborators. Jonson believed firmly that his should be the controlling mind. As he saw it, his task was both to devise the main idea of the masque, to which everything else should be subordinate, and to write the words in which the ideas found part of their expression. One of his best masques, for instance, is the comparatively early *Hymenaei*, of 1606. It was written for a marriage, and its central theme is union. Jonson very ingeniously makes many aspects of the entertainment illustrative of his theme. The seriousness with which he approached his task is revealed by his introductory remarks, where he says that things which are 'subjected to understanding'—that is, which make demands upon the intellect—have an advantage over 'those which are objected to sense'—that is, appeal only to the senses. The advantage is that 'the one sort are but momentary, and merely taking; the other impressing, and lasting: else the glory of all these solemnities had perished like a blaze, and gone out in the beholders' eyes, so short-lived are the bodies of all things, in comparison of their souls.' He goes on to explain that when he designs a masque there is something for the mind to grapple with, as well as more transitory attractions. The dominance of the soul over the body makes

> the most royal princes and greatest persons (who are
> commonly the personators of these actions) not only
> studious of riches and magnificence in the outward
> celebration or show, which rightly becomes them,
> but curious after the most high and hearty inventions
> to furnish the inward parts—and those grounded
> upon antiquity, and solid learnings—which, though
> their voice be taught to sound to present occasions,
> their sense or doth or should always lay hold on
> more removed mysteries.

It is the 'more removed mysteries' that he is concerned to provide; and he goes on to make plain that if his mysteries are so far removed as to be above the beholders' heads, that is their misfortune, not his. 'It is not my fault if I fill them out nectar and they run to metheglin.' In the performance of *Hymenaei* he was satisfied that everything had contributed to the total effect at which he had been aiming, so he was able to write:

> Such was the exquisite performance as, beside the pomp,
> splendour, or what we may call apparelling of such
> presentments, that alone, had all else been absent, was
> of power to surprise with delight, and steal away the
> spectators from themselves. Nor was there
> wanting whatsoever might give to the furniture or
> complement, either in riches or strangeness of the
> habits, delicacy of dances, magnificence of the scene,
> or divine rapture of music. Only the envy was that it
> lasted not still, or, now it is past, cannot by

imagination, much less description, be recovered to
a part of that spirit it had in the gliding by.

The printed text, he is well aware, is inadequate to
re-create the occasion, whether for those who were present
or those who were not.

Though in *Hymenaei* Jonson was satisfied with the
collaborative effort, as time went on he found it increasingly difficult to subdue himself to the medium, and
finally quarrelled with his chief collaborator, Inigo Jones.
Much of the success of the masques had been owing to
Jones's genius as a designer of costumes, scenes, and
machines. Fortunately many of his drawings survive to
assist our imaginations in reading the scripts. But Jonson
came to feel that Jones was too prominent, that the
masques were valued for their spectacular rather than
their intellectual and poetic appeal. Some masque writers
were able and willing to subordinate themselves to the
desire for spectacle. Samuel Daniel, for instance, writing
about his *Tethys' Festival*, seems to be trying to deflate
what he may have regarded as pretentiousness in Jonson,
for he says that 'in these things, wherein the only life
consists in show, the art and invention of the architect
gives the greatest grace, and is of most importance; ours
the least part and of least note in the time of the performance thereof; and therefore have I interserted the
description of the artificial part, which only speaks M.
Inigo Jones.'

In the twenty-five or so years during which Jonson was
the principal deviser of masques for the court he experi-
mented a good deal, partly no doubt because variety and
novelty were expected by the courtly audiences, which
must have been made up of very much the same individuals
from one occasion to the next. Throughout this time he

worked regularly and closely with Jones, but eventually a split came, and in his lines written about it, headed 'An Expostulation with Inigo Jones', Jonson reveals his anger and envy that Jones's contributions to masques have been preferred above his own.

> O shows, shows, mighty shows!
> The eloquence of masques! What need of prose,
> Or verse, or sense t'express immortal you?
> You are the spectacles of state! 'Tis true
> Court hieroglyphics! and all arts afford
> In the mere perspective of an inch board!

These lines were written in 1631; but it is clear that Jonson still has the same ideal of the essentials of the masque that he had expressed in the introduction to *Hymenaei* a quarter of a century before. Jones, he complains, demands spectators with

> Eyes that can pierce into the mysteries
> Of many colours, read them, and reveal
> Mythology there painted on slit deal!

For Jonson these are not sufficiently 'removed mysteries', and he continues with sarcasm, finding in Jones's popularity a symptom of the materialism of the age:

> Oh, to make boards to speak! There is a task!
> Painting and carpentry are the soul of masque—
> Pack with your peddling poetry to the stage—
> This is the money-get, mechanic age!

We are naturally inclined to sympathize with Jonson, but when Daniel wrote that the author's was 'the least part and of least note in the time of the performance thereof', he was not necessarily simply feigning humility in order to irritate Jonson.

There was in fact another collaborator in the success of a masque. This was the audience. Masques were given for particular audiences, even for particular individuals; and the spectators were also literally participants in the action. The culmination of the masque was the moment at which the masquers were revealed, preferably by some ingenious and spectacular device—it might be from within a shell, or a globe, or a mountain. These masquers, who then performed their dances, were on the same social level as the audience. They were of the aristocrats for whom the entertainment was devised, and they might include members of the royal family itself. This was the reason why masques were more or less unrepeatable events, which could not be put on for a season at the Blackfriars, as it were. Another reason was that the spectators, too, had to be aristocratic. For after the masquers had been revealed, and had performed their formal dances, they 'took out' partners from their audience, a fact which is often alluded to in the speeches and lyrics. Indeed there are some masques, of which *Hymenaei* is a notable example, which would lose much of their point if they were not performed before the sovereign himself. For many of the noble performers, it is hardly too much to say, the speeches and lyrics were likely to be little more than a mechanism by which a kind of Royal Ball was introduced and rounded off, however Ben Jonson might try to raise the tone of the occasion. And for many of the guests who thronged the private halls in which these events took place, much of the attraction was the wholly snobbish one of mingling with the great and watching them at their revels.

To say this is not to denigrate the work of those who wrote the scripts. But we shall not be able properly to appreciate their work unless we realize what it was intended to do, and unless we put ourselves in a position in which our imagination can at least partly supply that which is not provided by the printed page. Only then may we be able to show that Jonson was not entirely correct when he said that it 'cannot by imagination, much less description, be recovered to a part of that spirit it had in the gliding by'.

One possible advantage the reader of a masque may feel over its original spectators and participants is that, in so far as his imagination succeeds in recovering something of the spirit of the performance, it may do so on an ideal plane; for by no means every performance was as successful in the gliding by as Jonson considered *Hymenaei* to have been. Not all the skill of the poets and designers, musicians and dancers, could ensure success. There was a notable occasion in the same year as *Hymenaei* which seems to have been a total fiasco. It was given at Theobalds to celebrate the visit of the King of Denmark, the English Queen's brother. The script of the masque has not survived, so we cannot know precisely what was intended. What happened was wittily described by Sir John Harington:

> One day a great feast was held, and, after dinner, the representation of Solomon his temple and the coming of the Queen of Sheba was made or (as I may better say) was meant to have been made, before their majesties by device of the Earl of Salisbury and others. But alas! as all earthly things do fail to poor mortals in enjoyment, so did prove our presentment hereof. The lady who did play the Queen's part did carry most precious gifts to both their majesties, but, forgetting the steps arising to the canopy, overset her caskets into his Danish Majesty's lap, and fell at his feet—though I rather think it was in his face.

Much was the hurry and confusion—cloths and
napkins were at hand to make all clean. His Majesty
then got up and would dance with the Queen of Sheba.
But he fell down and humbled himself before her, and
was carried to an inner chamber and laid on a bed of
state, which was not a little defiled with the presents
of the Queen which had been bestowed on his
garments, such as wine, cream, jelly, beverage, cakes,
spices, and other good matters. The entertainment
and show went forward, and most of the presenters
went backward, or fell down, wine did so occupy
their upper chambers. Now did appear, in rich dress,
Hope, Faith, and Charity. Hope did essay to speak,
but wine rendered her endeavours so feeble that she
withdrew, and hoped the King would excuse her
brevity. Faith was then all alone—for I am certain
she was not joined with good works—and left the
Court in a staggering condition. Charity came to the
King's feet, and seemed to cover the multitude of
sins her sisters had committed. In some sort she made
obeisance and brought gifts, but said she would
return home again, as there was no gift which heaven
had not already given his Majesty. She then returned
to Hope and Faith, who were both sick and spewing
in the lower hall. Next came Victory in bright
armour, and presented a rich sword to the King, who
did not accept it, but put it by with his hand; and,
by a strange medley of versification, did endeavour
to make suit to the King. But Victory did not
triumph long, for, after much lamentable utterance,
she was led away like a silly captive, and laid to sleep
in the outer steps of the ante-chamber. Now did
Peace make entry and strive to get foremost to the
King; but I grieve to tell how great wrath she did

discover unto those of her attendants, and much
contrary to her semblance, most rudely made war
with her olive branch, and laid on the pates of those
who did oppose her coming.

One feature of the entertainment which is amply
brought out in Harington's description and was not unique
to this occasion, though it is never mentioned in the
scripts of masques, is the lavishness of the hospitality. The
consumption of food and drink was often on the same
scale of extravagance as everything else.

Masques on the printed page

Although Jonson and other authors of masques were aware
that the printing of the texts could not do justice to the
magnificence of the occasions, they allowed this to happen,
realizing no doubt that this was the only way to salvage
anything for posterity. Jonson wrote in the Preface to his
first masque: 'The honour and splendour of these spec-
tacles was such in the performance, as, could those hours
have lasted, this of mine now had been a most unprofit-
able work.' In the attempt at reclamation he and some of
his fellows sometimes added descriptive passages to the
printed versions in the effort to convey a sense of the
occasion. Some of Jonson's masques, indeed, are printed
with remarkable amplitude of annotation and comment in
his most idiosyncratic and revealing prose. What seems
sometimes to have happened is that before the masque was
performed a simple text was printed. It may have been
used by the performers to learn their parts, but probably
was intended mainly as a kind of souvenir programme
for the participants and guests. A clear example is provided by a little masque of Jonson's called *Lovers Made*

Men, a charming but unambitious specimen written not for a royal audience but for a nobleman wishing to offer a memorable entertainment to a visiting ambassador. It has special significance in that it is the first English dramatic text which we know to have been entirely set to music —the innovation of recitative was employed. For this reason it is sometimes referred to as the first English opera. Unfortunately the original music has not been preserved.

There survives, in the Bodleian Library, one copy of the printed text dated 1617, the year of performance. It was obviously printed for private use, since the title page mentions neither author, printer, nor publisher. Even this text contains quite long descriptive passages. Jonson may be implicitly acknowledging that even those present at the performance required help in order to understand the significance of the figures in the proscenium arch, 'on the top of which', we are told, 'Humanity, placed in figure, sits with her lap full of flowers, scattering them with her right hand, and holding a golden chain in her left, to show both the freedom, and the bond of courtesy; with this inscription: *Super omnia vultus*'. The directions, or descriptions of the action, are in the present tense. This masque was reprinted in the Second Folio of Jonson's *Works*, of 1640-41, in a version which was slightly revised by Jonson. There is an interesting insertion: Jonson adds a mention of one piece of action, and the information that 'the whole Masque was sung after the Italian manner, *stilo recitativo*, by Master Nicholas Lanier, who ordered and made both the Scene and the music.' Moreover the descriptions are altered from the present to the past tense.

In *Lovers Made Men* Jonson did not feel impelled to add much information, partly no doubt because the original quarto had clear descriptions of the action, and partly because this was not a spectacular masque. But the change in the tense of the descriptions gives us a clue to the changes made in other masques in order to make them suitable for reading. An example is Campion's *The Lords' Masque*, published as *The Description, Speeches and Songs of The Lords' Masque presented in the Banqueting House on the marriage night of the high and mighty Count Palatine and the royally descended the Lady Elizabeth. 14 February 1613*. Campion has added passages which aim at describing something of what was seen, and even the music that was heard. There is, for example, an anti-masque, for which the original direction seems to have read, 'at the sound of strange music twelve Frantics enter, six men and six women, all presented in sundry habits and humours'. Probably the precise details of the Frantics were not decided till the masque was put into rehearsal. Anyhow the description of them reads like an addition:

> There was the Lover, the Self-Lover, the Melancholic Man full of fear, the School-man over-come with fantasy, the over-watched Usurer, with others that made an absolute medley of madness; in midst of whom Entheus (or Poetic Fury) was hurried forth and tossed up and down, till by virtue of a new change in the music the Lunatics fell into a mad measure, fitted to a loud fantastic tune; but in the end thereof the music changed into a very solemn air, which they softly played while Orpheus spake.

Similarly Campion added for the reader descriptions of costume, of action, and of spectacle. Indeed he includes a tribute to the work of Inigo Jones in connexion with a passage which well illustrates the close intermingling of the arts in the masque form. The masque's very fable is concerned with this. Orpheus releases Entheus from the dominions of madness, in which he has mistakenly been imprisoned, and pays tribute to his power:

> For thy excelling rapture, ev'n through things
> That seem most light, is borne with sacred wings:
> Nor are these musics, shows, or revels vain,
> When thou adornest them with thy Phoebean brain.

He therefore has, he says, been commanded by Jove to call on Entheus

> to create
> Inventions rare, this night to celebrate,
> Such as become a nuptial by his will
> Begun and ended.

Thus the masque reflects the actual situation, Jove standing for James I, Entheus for Campion as poet, and Orpheus for Campion as composer. Entheus calls on Prometheus (whose function resembles that of Inigo Jones) to show 'his stars to our stars', and they are summoned and described in a mixture of solo and choric song. The reader learns that 'in clouds of several colours ... appeared eight Stars of extraordinary bigness, which so were placed as that they seemed to be fixed between the firmament and the earth'. Prometheus agrees to share with Orpheus and Entheus responsibility for the masque: which is as much as to say that spectacle, represented by Prometheus, will join with music (Orpheus), and poetry (Entheus), 'in equal balance'. He explains that he has stealthily brought from heaven eight stars, which after they have performed a choral dance will turn into human figures. There follows a song directing the movements of the stars. Most unfortunately the music has not survived, but obviously the design is admirable, and to judge by Campion's description was well carried out. He tells us that

according to the humour of this song, the Stars moved
in an exceeding strange and delightful manner, and I
suppose few have ever seen more neat artifice than Master
Inigo Jones showed in contriving their motion, who
in all the rest of the workmanship which belonged
to the whole invention showed extraordinary
industry and skill, which if it be not as lively expressed
in writing as it appeared in view, rob not him of his
due, but lay the blame on my want of right
apprehending his instructions for the adorning of his
art.

Masque writers were conscious of the fragility of their
art, which was indeed one of its attractions. *The Lords'
Masque* is one that has worn well and is comparatively
easy to read, partly because of the amplitude and skill of
Campion's descriptive writing, and partly because it has
a very well-developed literary framework. But even here
we have to manage without the music and dances, and
so can get only a partial impression of the effect. It is a
masque in which the co-operation of all concerned seems
—so far as we know—to have been ideal. They did indeed
work, as Prometheus says, 'in equal balance'. Yet only
the poet's work has survived. What we know of his
collaborators' efforts we know through him. The result
is that we have an imperfect knowledge of his work, too.

Eye-witness accounts of dramatic performances during
the Elizabethan and Jacobean period are rare. There were
no professional theatre critics, and surviving letters and
diaries only occasionally mention visits to the theatre. But
performances of masques were special occasions, worth
writing home about. We have comments on some of them,
and detailed descriptions of a few. One of which a particularly interesting description survives is Jonson's *Plea-*

sure Reconciled to Virtue, which therefore provides an exceptional opportunity to consider the difference between the impression a masque may make on us as we read, and the impression it made in performance, So I should like to look at this masque in some detail, trying first to suggest something of the impression we might have of it from the printed page, and then looking at surviving descriptions of the occasion itself.

The script of Pleasure Reconciled to Virtue

It was printed in the Second Folio of Jonson's *Works*, which appeared in 1640-41, and is there headed *Pleasure Reconciled to Virtue: A Masque as it was presented at Court before King James, 1618*. Its basic idea, or device, is contained in the emblem of Hercules at the crossroads, required to choose between Virtue and Vice (or Pleasure). It was a well-known idea, often illustrated in emblem-books. Jonson gives it a certain dramatic movement by imagining the reconciliation of Pleasure and Virtue in common opposition to Vice. The setting is Mount Atlas, and the text begins with a description of the 'scene', which represented 'the mountain Atlas, who had his top ending in the figure of an old man'. At his feet was 'a grove of ivy ... out of which, to a wild music of cymbals, flutes, and tabors was brought forth Comus, the god of cheer or the belly, riding in triumph....' An attendant went before him, bearing Hercules's bowl, while others sang a 'hymn'. This is in rhymed couplets, and is a fine, vigorous celebration of Comus as the god of the belly. It is followed by a long prose speech from the bowl-bearer in a vigorous, not to say coarse, style that would be perfectly at home in one of Jonson's London comedies. He suggests that the singers are wasting their

time, 'for where did you ever read or hear that the belly
had any ears?' Behind this lies a hint of allegory, suggesting the mindlessness of mere sensual gratification, but
it is given with no sign of didacticism—the bowl-bearer
declares, 'I am all for the belly', though admittedly only
after saying that he has 'drunk like a frog today'. During his
speech he says, 'I would have a Tun now brought in to
dance, and so many bottles about him', and explains that
'men that drink hard, and serve the belly in any place of
quality ... can transform themselves, and do every day,
to Bottles or Tuns when they please.'

After his speech comes the laconic direction, 'here the
first Anti-masque, after which Hercules'. For the reader,
then, there is no information about what the anti-masque
represented beyond what he may deduce from what has
gone before and from Hercules's speech (in rhymed couplets) which follows. Hercules exclaims at the 'monsters'
he has seen, saying:

> these are sponges, and not men:
> Bottles? Mere vessels? Half a ton of paunch?

He is shocked at what he sees; indeed he moralizes seriously
on the spectacle, rebuking whatever it is that he has seen,
and drawing the general comment:

> Can this be pleasure, to extinguish man,
> Or so quite change him in his figure? Can
> The belly love his pain, and be content
> With no delight but what's a punishment?

He is, in fact, moralizing on the self-destructive quality
of sensual indulgence. He commands the grove from
which Comus had appeared to vanish, and then the
musicians are revealed, and the chorus invites Hercules
to rest awhile from his mighty labour whilst Virtue,

> for whose sake
> Thou dost this godlike travail take,
> May of the choicest herbage make
> (Here on this mountain bred)
>   A crown, a crown
> For thy immortal head.

Then followed the second anti-masque, about which the description tells us merely that it 'was of Pigmies'. It begins with a brief and brilliant passage of dialogue in which the pigmies reveal their resentment that Hercules has just killed their leader, Antaeus, and in which they plan to kill him. Confident that he is in their power, they dance for joy; but he is woken by the chorus, and at a look from him the pigmies 'ran into holes'. Mercury then 'descended from the hill, with a garland of poplar to crown him'. The presentation is made during the course of a long eulogy of Hercules in which Mercury praises him for his conquest of Antaeus and 'the voluptuous Comus'.

The symbolism behind the pigmies is not as clear as that behind Comus and the barrels, but they have been plausibly interpreted as representatives of a kind of pleasure deriving from absurd over-confidence in one's own powers. This moral, however, has to be drawn by the reader.

Mercury tells Hercules that the time has come for peace to be made between Virtue and Pleasure, and that both should meet

> here in the sight
> Of Hesperus, the glory of the west,
> The brightest star, that from his burning crest
> Lights all on this side the Atlantic seas.

This unmistakably stands for King James, who was present at the masque, and the use of an allegorical name —Hesperus—for him means that he is virtually a character in the action, even though he has no function to perform beyond being present. The main masque is foreshadowed as Mercury tells that

> Pleasure, for his delight,
> Is reconciled to Virtue; and this night
> Virtue brings forth twelve Princes have been bred
> In this rough mountain, and near Atlas' head,
> The hill of knowledge; one, and chief, of whom
> Of the bright race of Hesperus is come,
> Who shall in time the same that he is be,
> And now is only a less light than he.

This is, of course, King James's son, Prince Charles, later to become King Charles I. He and the other princes, we are told, are to be trusted with pleasure under the control of virtue. Their training in the 'rough mountain' has fitted them to withstand temptation. Another choral song, calling forth the twelve masquers from the mountain, opens with one of Jonson's less happy invocations:

> Ope, aged Atlas, open then thy lap,
> And from thy beamy bosom strike a light....

It goes on to make explicit the moral point that the young men are sufficiently trained by Virtue to be incapable of corruption by Pleasure:

> They who are bred
>   Within the hill
>   Of skill
> May safely tread
>   What path they will:
> No ground of good is hollow.

In their descent from the hill the masquers are led by 'Daedalus, the wise'. While they 'put themselves in form' —that is, line up for the dance—he is instructed to sing a song which gives instructions for the dance and which allegorizes it, suggesting that the lines of the dance will first stand for the uncertain stage at which youth should pause for a time while deciding whether to follow the influence of Pleasure or of Virtue. Men will be able to admire what Daedalus calls the 'wisdom' of the dancers' feet. He presents an idealized and elevated view of the function of dance, claiming it as an exercise which

> Not only shows the mover's wit,
> But maketh the beholder wise,
> As he hath power to rise to it.

Then come instructions for two more dances, each followed by a song from Daedalus. The second song exhorts the dancers to greater endeavours, this time in the service of beauty, which they are to create in their dance, which is the 'labyrinth of beauty', and which will be watched by the beautiful women spectators—again the audience is referred to.

The song suggesting the wisdom of the dance has been followed by one seeing the dance as an emblem of beauty. Now Daedalus leads the dancers into what he calls 'the subtlest maze of all; that's love'. He instructs the masquers to choose their partners from the audience; and he does so in a most felicitous image:

> Go, choose among, but with a mind
> As gentle as the stroking wind
> Runs o'er the gentler flowers.

This, too, is moralized; for the dancers are told:

> Grace, laughter, and discourse may meet,
>   And yet the beauty go not less;
> For what is noble should be sweet,
>   But not dissolved in wantonness.

After this song the masquers 'danced with the Ladies, and the whole Revels followed'. This was by far the longest part of the evening's festivities, though in the reading it occupies us for only a second. The masque has a brief but impressive-sounding coda; for we are told that after the 'revels' Mercury spoke verses which were 'repeated in song by two Trebles, two Tenors, a Bass, and the whole Chorus'. The dancers are invited to reflect on what they have been doing, and to consider that the hours they have spent with Pleasure were spared to them by Virtue. 'But', they are told,

> ... she will have you know
>   That though
> Her sports be soft, her life is hard.

So he instructs the masquers to 'return unto the hill' and so labour there in the course of virtue that they

> ever may look down
> Upon triumphed Chance.

In darkness Virtue shines, constantly improving herself, and her seat is in the mountains. The last lines of the masque are austere, and far from sycophantic considering that they are addressed primarily to Prince Charles:

> There, there is Virtue's seat.
> Strive to keep her your own;
>   'Tis only she can make you great,
> Though place here make you known.

After which they danced their last dance [and] returned into the scene, which closed, and was a Mountain again, as before.

Pleasure Reconciled to Virtue can be quickly read. In print it occupies only about ten pages. From the reading we have the impression of a very serious work of considerable allegorical power. We can admire various facets of Jonson's art: the vigour of his introductory couplets, the mastery of colloquial prose displayed in the Bowl-bearer's speech, the skill in verse dialogue of the brief episode of the pigmies, the dignity, variety, and grace of the lyric measures. These are largely literary virtues. As we consider the piece in relation to the instructions for action and dances we may feel, too, that it was ingeniously devised to permit the display of various non-literary arts: instrumental music, solo and choral song, symbolic choreography, scenic spectacle, and so on. Considering the occasion—Prince Charles's first masque—we can admire the overall constructive power which has created an appropriate device, complimentary yet far from sycophantic, graceful yet with real substance.

Pleasure Reconciled to Virtue *in performance*

We can then turn to eye-witness accounts of the occasion to which Jonson contributed. It happens that a remarkably detailed account of *Pleasure Reconciled to Virtue* has survived. It is given in a letter written to Venice by Orazio Busino, who was chaplain to the Venetian Embassy. He wrote in Italian; and it is clear from his account of the masque that his English was imperfect. We should not, then, attach too much importance to his lack of appreciation of the masque's literary merits. It is interesting, still,

to see where he puts his emphases. He begins by remarking on the great number of theatrical representations
given in London throughout the year, and the colourful
clothes of the crowds who attend them. Similarly during
the Christmas season the Court enjoys a series of banquets,
plays, and masques, of which the most prominent is performed on Twelfth Night, when 'a large hall is fitted up
like a theatre, with well-secured boxes all round. The stage
is at one end, and his Majesty's chair in front under an
ample canopy.' He tells that the ambassador had been
'invited to see a representation and masque, which had
been prepared with extraordinary pains, the chief performer being the King's own son and heir, the Prince of
Wales, now seventeen years old, an agile youth, handsome
and very graceful'. The ambassador's party went early to
the hall, and though the ambassador himself was privately
entertained until the beginning of the performance the
members of his retinue were shown to a box where they
were uncomfortably crowded and extremely resentful
because the master of ceremonies also allowed into the
box a Spaniard, who 'placed himself more comfortably
than any of us'. Busino describes how, waiting for the
King, they admired 'the decorations and beauty of the
house', which he describes in some detail. He admired,
too, the ladies in the audience. 'Every box', he says,

> was filled notably with most noble and richly
> arrayed ladies, in number some 600 and more
> according to the general estimate; the dresses being
> of such variety in cut and colour as to be inde-
> scribable; the most delicate plumes over their heads,
> springing from their foreheads or in their hands
> serving as fans; strings of jewels on their necks
> and bosoms and in their girdles and apparel in

such quantity that they looked like so many
queens, so that at the beginning, with but little
light, such as that of the dawn or of the evening
twilight, the splendour of their diamonds and other
jewels was so brilliant that they looked like so
many stars. During the two hours of waiting we
had leisure to examine them again and again.

Unfortunately Busino was short-sighted, so had to rely
on his companions for reports of the appearance of the
court ladies. Though they found many to admire, 'they
came to the conclusion that amongst much grain there
was also a mixture of husk and straw, that is to say,
shrivelled women and some very devoted to Saint Charles,
but that the beauties outnumbered them'. Their costume
he reported as conveniently serving 'as a blind to nature's
defects', and he noted that 'the plump and buxom display
their bosoms very liberally, and those who are lean go
muffled up to the throat'.

After a couple of hours of waiting, the King appeared
with the Spanish and Venetian ambassadors—because of
a quarrel about precedence, the French ambassador was
not present. Fifteen or twenty brass instruments sounded
a fanfare, and the royal party seated itself. The body of
the hall was cleared by the Lord Chamberlain, 'and in
the middle of the theatre there appeared a fine and spacious
area carpeted all over with green cloth'. And the masque
began.

Partly no doubt because of the language difficulty,
Busino's description is largely concerned with what he
saw, rather than heard. It gives us some information that
we could not have gleaned from the text. After the painted
curtains had dropped, 'there appeared first of all Mount
Atlas, whose enormous head was alone visible up aloft

under the very roof of the theatre'. We learn from Busino that it was mechanically contrived in such a way that 'it rolled up its eyes and moved itself very cleverly'. The hymn sung to Comus by his attendants seems to have been inadequately performed. Busino says that 'a very chubby Bacchus [that is, Comus] appeared on a car drawn by four gownsmen, who sang in an undertone before his Majesty'. He found the whole of the first scene 'very gay and burlesque'. He is informative about the anti-masquers, telling us that, of the first set, one 'was in a barrel, all but his extremities, his companions being similarly cased in huge wicker flasks, very well made. They danced awhile to the sound of the cornets and trumpets, performing various and most extravagant antics.' In the second anti-masque he refers to 'a gigantic man representing Hercules with his club, who strove with Antaeus and performed other feats'. There is no indication in the text that Hercules's conquest of Antaeus was to be represented, though the fact that it was adds considerably to the First Pigmy's first line, which is 'Antaeus dead, and Hercules yet live?' It is from Busino, too, that we learn that the pigmies were 'twelve masked boys in the guise of frogs'. Busino gives us a variety of details about the spectacle employed, though sometimes he admits to a lack of comprehension. He saw, for example, 'a number of singers, dressed in long red gowns to represent high priests ... wearing gilt mitres. In the midst of them was a goddess in a long white robe, and they sang some jigs which we did not understand.' He describes in detail the anti-masquers' costumes, and their dances, and gives us a vivid account of an entirely unrehearsed episode:

> Last of all they danced the Spanish dance, one at
> a time, each with his lady, and being well nigh

tired they began to lag, whereupon the King,
who is naturally choleric, got impatient and
shouted aloud 'Why don't they dance? What did
they make me come here for? Devil take you all,
dance!' Upon this the Marquis of Buckingham,
his Majesty's favourite, immediately sprang
forward, cutting a score of lofty and very minute
capers, with so much grace and agility that he
not only appeased the ire of his angry lord, but
rendered himself the admiration and delight of
everybody. The other masquers, thus encouraged,
continued to exhibit their prowess one after
another with various ladies, also finishing with
capers and lifting their goddesses from the ground.

After this all went well, and at the end of the masque

the Prince went in triumph to kiss his father's
hands. The King embraced and kissed him tenderly, and
then honoured the Marquis with marks of extraordinary
affection, patting his face. The King now rose from
his chair, took the ambassadors along with him,
and after passing through a number of chambers
and galleries he reached a hall where the usual
collation was spread for the performers, a light
being carried before him. After he had glanced
all round the table he departed, and forthwith the
parties concerned pounced upon the prey like so
many harpies. The table was covered almost entirely
with seasoned pasties and very few sugar confec-
tions. There were some large figures, but they were
of painted pasteboard for ornament. The repast
was served upon glass plates or dishes and at
the first assault they upset the table and the crash
of glass platters reminded me precisely of a severe

hailstorm at Midsummer sma_hing the window
glass. The story ended at half-past two in the
morning and half-disgusted and weary we
returned home.

He ends his letter with: 'Should your lordships writhe
on reading or listening to this tediousness you may
imagine the weariness I feel in relating it.'

It is unfortunate that this account, full, detailed, and
intelligent though it is, should have come from a foreigner
with limited understanding of the language in which the
masque was written. Busino was a kind of political obser-
ver, with a strong professional interest in the social aspects
of the scene. But in this he was not untypical. The masque
writer was faced with an audience which was a far cry
from the literary-minded readers who may read and enjoy
the printed text today. Those whom he had to try to
please must have looked upon the performance very
largely as a social occasion of great magnitude, scarcely
at all as an aesthetic and philosophical stimulus. This
particular masque occasioned disappointment even among
those fully capable of understanding it. Sir Edward Sher-
burn's criticism suggests that he did not find it adequate
in its glorification of Prince Charles: 'It came far short
of the expectation, and Master Inigo Jones hath lost in
his reputation in regard some extraordinary device was
looked for, it being the Prince's first masque, and a poorer
was never seen.' Novelty of device in revealing the
masquers had been expected as the highspot of the occasion but was not supplied. Nathaniel Brent wrote to Sir
Dudley Carleton: 'The masque on Twelfth Night is not
commended of any. The poet is grown so dull that his
device is not worth the relating, much less the copying
out. Divers think he should return to his old trade of

bricklaying again.' John Chamberlain also found that 'there was nothing in it extraordinary, but rather the invention proved dull'. But he had some consolation: 'Master Controller's daughter bare away the bell for delicate dancing, though remarkable for nothing else but the multitude of jewels wherewith she was hanged as it were all over.' And Sir Edward Harwood, though he found 'the conceit good', thought 'the poetry not so'.

The nature of the masque

It may appear, then, that while a reading of the masque will not give us anything like the experience that Jonson aimed at creating, to have been present at the performance would have been unlikely to do so, either. At the performance, too much must have been beyond the author's control. He could not ensure that his words were given full value, even that they were not swamped by the music—though the danger of this may well have been the reason for his instruction that the final song should be spoken before it was sung. He could not govern the reactions of the spectators during the dances, nor anticipate the King's splenetic outburst, which seems likely to have had an effect on the spectators, too, and which must have made it difficult for the performers to re-create the proper mood for the masque's closing episode.

Yet when we read, too, we must acknowledge that much even of what was designed, or at least approved, by the author lies outside our grasp. The mimed fight of Hercules with Antaeus, for example, of which Busino writes, must have been integral to the masque's action, but is not mentioned in the printed text.

Where, then, does the true masque exist? We might say, only in the author's imagination. Or we might feel that the performance as given, however it differed from the author's conceptions, was nevertheless the thing itself in that a work of art exists only in realization, and not in intention. We might claim that it exists best in the mind of the reader, supplied with the fullest possible amount of background information and endowed with a sympathetic imagination. But perhaps the fairest answer would be that a masque—and we might extend this to any other performed work of art—exists somewhere between the imagined and the realized, the intention and the result; that the intention itself is only partial, that the artist must allow for the unexpected and be content with imperfection of realization. More than most playwrights, the masque-writer was dependent upon his collaborators, both those who performed and those who, as the French say, 'assisted' with their presence. I have concentrated on the writers of masques and their products because masques are extreme examples of works of quasi-theatrical art which are worth reading, but which in the reading must create an impression very different from that towards which the writer was consciously contributing. The script offers us some rather disjointed fragments which are all that can be preserved of the original. To contemplate the difference between the script and, so far as we can imagine it, the occasion, may help us to realize the less extreme but still appreciable difference between the script of a play and the performed effect.

Script and performance

The discrepancies between script and reports of perform-ances explored in this chapter merely represent in a rather extreme form a state that obtains in relation to dramatic literature of every kind and period. A similar study might be made of, for example, some of the Shakespeare adaptations that were made during a period when the influence of the masques was making itself felt on the popular theatre. It is difficult for us to take Nahum Tate's version of *King Lear* seriously, at any rate on the printed page; yet it held the stage successfully for close on two hundred years. That it was preferred to Shakespeare's original play may be accounted for partly as a vagary of taste, but may be referred also to basic theatrical qualities that are not to be despised in any period. Colley Cibber's adaptation of *Richard III*, made in 1700, had an even longer stage life, and is still sometimes defended as a more effectively theatrical work than that on which it is based. The contribution of the individual performer unassisted by theatrical paraphernalia may be gauged by considering the printed speeches made by great orators in relation to accounts of the effect they had when they were delivered. Garrick's Ode, written for the Shakespeare Jubilee in 1769, is an interesting example, which happens to have been delivered as well as written by a great actor. It reads thinly, yet accounts of the occasion at which it was given show beyond dispute that with it Garrick created an immensely thrilling and moving effect. The contribution of the theatre and all that the use of a 'live' medium implies is evident in the discrepancy between the impact not merely of the script but also of the film version in comparison with actual performances of, for instance, Peter Brook's production of the *Marat-Sade* play. Fully to investigate these matters would require a study of acting techniques and the psychology of audiences. For the student of literature the point that may emerge from such comparisons is the desirability that scripts intended for performance should be approached with an openness that allows for effects not explicit in what is written, and consequently also for variety of interpretation.

4

The critical problem

The equipment of the critic

In Chapter Two an attempt was made to demonstrate that the conventions governing the printing of play-scripts do little to help the communication of the theatrical experience that they nominally represent; and in Chapter Three a printed text was compared with accounts of the performance based upon it, in the attempt to show how different is the experience of a reader from that of a spectator. From this it should be clear that the reader of a play-script needs to bring to his task expectations different from those he would bring to works of pure literature. He must himself supply that extra dimension that in the theatre the performers must add in order to bring the work to its full realization. And if his imagination does not work on a theatrical plane, he is in danger of serious misreading. The purpose of this final chapter is to explore some of the implications of this situation as it affects critics and readers.

Marlowe's critics and The Jew of Malta

The academic critic is frequently accused of showing too

little concern for a play's theatrical effect, and there is a real danger that he will under-rate plays in which theatrical virtues are more prominent than literary ones. A production by the Royal Shakespeare Company effectively demonstrated the merits of a play that had suffered a long period of neglect. The play was Marlowe's *The Jew of Malta*, which had often been regarded as one of the weakest of its author's works. It had been felt to lack unity of tone and to lapse into incoherence in the second act. It is only fair to say that the play had been neglected much more in the theatre than in the study. Academic critics had not been given the chance to see it performed, for though it had been one of the most popular plays in the Elizabethan repertory, the Royal Shakespeare Company's performances, first given in London in 1964, were the first of any importance that the play had had since Edmund Kean played Barabbas in the early nineteenth century. This is not, then, a case of academic critics wilfully looking in the face of a play's theatrical success and refusing to grant its merit on irrelevant grounds. Even before this production a number of critics—such as Harry Levin, Leo Kirschbaum, J. C. Maxwell, and G. K. Hunter —had taken the play seriously in writings that might well have encouraged those who present plays to take a risk with this one. Its rehabilitation may be traced as far back as 1920, when T. S. Eliot claimed that if we take the play 'as a farce, the concluding act becomes intelligible.... It is the farce of the old English humour, the terribly serious, even savage comic humour....' Still the play continued to have a bad press in some quarters. F. P. Wilson, for example—one of Marlowe's best critics—said, in a book published in 1953:

There is little in the first two acts that could have

been written by any other man: in the last three
there is very little that could not have come from
the pen of another writer—and a small writer
at that.... To suppose that the same man who
wrote the first two acts was wholly responsible
for the last three is revolting to sense and sensibility,
for these belong to a different world of art, if
indeed they can be said to belong to the world
of art at all.

Critics have felt uncertain about the play's tone, and
so did those who were to perform it. With no traditions
of performance to follow or even to disagree with, they
were working in a void, and it was not until they faced
the first-night audience that they discovered how the play
would go. The result was a theatrical success, and a vindi-
cation of Marlowe's dramatic technique in this play.
Episodes which in reading seem thin and underwritten
were revealed as theatrically workable. An example is the
passage in which Ferneze and Katharine learn of and
mourn the deaths of their sons, who have killed one
another in a duel deliberately engineered by Barabbas.
It runs:

Ferneze. What sight is this? My Lodovico slain?
   These arms of mine shall be thy sepulchre.

Katharine. Who is this? My son Mathias slain!

Ferneze. O Lodowick, hadst thou perish'd by the Turk,
   Wretched Ferneze might have veng'd thy
   death!

Katharine. Thy son slew mine, and I'll revenge his death.

Ferneze. Look, Katharine, look! Thy son gave mine
   these wounds.

Katharine. O, leave to grieve me! I am griev'd enough.

Ferneze. O, that my sighs could turn to lively breath,
And these my tears to blood, that he might
live!

Katharine. Who made them enemies?

Ferneze. I know not; and that grieves me most of all.

Katharine. My son loved thine,

Ferneze. And so did Lodowick him.

Katharine. Lend me that weapon that did kill my son,
And it shall murder me.

Ferneze. Nay, madam, stay; that weapon was my son's,
And on that rather should Ferneze die.

Katharine. Hold: let's enquire the causers of their deaths,
That we may venge their blood upon their
heads.

Ferneze. Then take them up, and let them be interr'd
Within one sacred monument of stone;
Upon which altar I will offer up
My daily sacrifice of sighs and tears,
And with my prayers pierce impartial heavens,
Till they [reveal] the causers of our smarts,
Which forced theirs hands divide united hearts.
Come, Katharine; our losses equal are,
Then of true grief let us take equal share.

That encompasses a remarkable amount of action and

emotion within a short space, and of course it does not give full verbal expression to the emotion. A novelist would be likely to need much more space in which to portray the surprise and grief of the parents on seeing their sons slain, their desire for vengeance, their enquiry into the circumstances, their mourning impulse to suicide, their determination to seek out the truth and pursue vengeance, and Ferneze's tribute to the boys' memory. A naturalistic playwright, too, might have developed the situation in much greater detail. Yet Marlowe's stylized and foreshortening technique worked perfectly in the theatre because it was performed in a manner that enabled us to accept these speeches less as expressions of the characters' feelings than as stylized pointers to a complex emotional situation. At 'What sight is this?' Ferneze was kneeling by his son's body. Katharine entered at the back of the stage, moved forwards, and knelt by her son's body. Her attitude was thus parallel to Ferneze's. At first, both parents were conscious only of their dead sons. Their grief was expressed as much by their anguished move-ments, their subdued tones, and their postures as by their words. At 'Thy son slew mine' Katharine faced Ferneze. The tone of their ensuing duologue was of bitter grief. At 'Lend me that weapon' Katharine rose and moved across to Ferneze, and one of the Knights of Malta, who had been shocked spectators, approached Katharine as if in readiness to restrain her from killing herself. Other Knights followed him. Katharine held up her hands at 'Hold: let's enquire the causers of their deaths'. Ferneze stood as he said 'Then take them up', and moved towards Katharine. The Knights came further forward and posi-tioned themselves three beside each of the bodies, which they then raised in formal fashion and supported on their shoulders. Katharine moved to the centre of the stage, and then forward to Ferneze's right. The parents were now at the front of the stage, their sons' uplifted bodies, each supported by three Knights, further upstage. At 'Come, Katharine', Ferneze and Katharine joined hands, united in grief. A funeral march sounded as they followed the Knights slowly bearing the bodies off the stage.

It was thus revealed that, given sympathetic treatment, Marlowe's dialogue was perfectly adequate, not as a literary expression of a situation, but as one element in its theatrical realization. Movements, music, silences, gestures, facial expressions, the reactions of spectators, the tones of voice in which the speeches were given, all made their contribution, and all were such as the playwright is entitled to expect from his interpreters. Marlowe's stylized and foreshortening technique was fully justified. This was not a case of the actors *adding* their creation to that of the playwright. Rather they had found how he ought to be played. We cannot, of course, say for certain that this is how Marlowe himself would have directed the scene. But the fact that it was successful when played thus, with no adventitious aids, must make us fairly confident that Marlowe knew what he was doing.

To go through the whole play in similar detail would be tedious. Other passages which on the printed page seem equally underwritten were equally successful on the stage. The play went with great pace and was revealed as one of complex irony, tragic in structure but comic in tone. The critic of *The Times* rightly described the production as 'a classic demonstration of how far a play's theatrical impact can differ from the impression it makes on the page'. It is still possible for critics to dislike Marlowe's play, but they can no longer justifiably doubt its theatrical viability, and they are far less likely to question its potential unity of impact.

That the characteristics of *The Jew of Malta* described here are typical of Marlowe is suggested by a passage from Glynne Wickham's book, *Shakespeare's Dramatic Heritage* (1969). In a chapter called 'Notes on the Staging of Marlowe's Plays', he writes:

Events are telescoped with frenzied haste. In consequence the reader of these plays gains the impression that they are poorly constructed, oscillating unevenly between rhetorical scenes of sustained poetic brilliance combined with perceptive character delineation on the one hand and sketchy linking devices on the other. Literary criticism knows no way round this difficulty. I venture to suggest that the opera critic would know better; for few indeed are the operatic librettos which follow any other pattern; and what, in the libretto, looks like a lazy linking device takes on an altogether different air in the theatre when filled out with its full orchestral accompaniment. So too, where Marlowe is concerned, I think we must make greater allowance than is usually admitted for the ritualistic quality of the theatre in which he worked. The coming and goings of his princes, lords and captains which in the text *read* bleakly enough, take on a very different character *on the stage* when seen in their full context of costume, colour and movement. Absorbed as we are in this spectacle, shifting and changing solemnly or kaleidoscopically before our eyes, we have not time to notice, let alone to ponder, the abruptness of a change of locale or the short-circuiting of time itself. All this provides the orchestration which underlies the verbal linking of one great aria to the next.

There an academic critic who is also a practical man of the theatre offers his testimony to the theatrical qualities of plays that have sometimes been regarded as over-literary.

The difficulty of reading *The Jew of Malta* in a manner that made allowance for the way it was likely to work in the theatre must be felt to be one of the reasons why it has been so underrated that for well over a century it fell out of the repertory. Of course, sheer accident—as well as economics—plays a large part. It is not economically possible for all the good plays written in English to be available in performance at one and the same time, or indeed for them all to be performed even once in a generation. There may be many plays that are seriously underrated and will remain so in the absence of sympathetic performance. The Royal Shakespeare Company did another admirable job of resuscitation on *The Revenger's Tragedy*, and will no doubt go on discovering the merits of plays that have been little performed. It is also possible that a real spate of productions of Elizabethan and Jacobean plays might cause something of a shift of evaluation even of those that have been performed. Two that have received more attention than most are Webster's *The White Devil* and *The Duchess of Malfi*, and there are times when I suspect that, superbly written as they are, they owe their comparative popularity on the stage rather to their literary than to their overall theatrical merits.

Some untheatrical readings

The reading of plays in an untheatrical way can, then, help to contribute to their neglect in the professional theatre and to their under-valuation. It can also result in distortion in critical accounts of them. We are here, of course, in an entirely subjective realm. What seems to one person to be a distortion may seem to another to be a revelation. Still, it is possible to give blatant examples, even sometimes from very theatrically-minded critics. Jan Kott, for example, has worked in the professional theatre as a producer, yet he can write about *A Midsummer Night's Dream* in terms that seem quite incapable of theatrical realization, at least without serious distortion of the text. This is, he says in *Shakespeare Our Contemporary*, 'the most erotic of Shakespeare's plays'. He imagines Titania's court 'consisting of old men and women, toothless and shaking, their mouths wet with saliva, who sniggeringly procure a monster for their mistress'. He finds Oberon is determined that his Queen shall sleep with a beast of a kind which represents 'abundant sexual potency.... Bottom is eventually transformed into an ass. But in this nightmarish summer night, the ass does not symbolize stupidity. Since antiquity and up to the Renaissance the ass was credited with the strongest sexual potency and among all the quadrupeds is supposed to have the longest and hardest phallus.' And he goes on: 'I visualize Titania as a very tall, flat and fair girl, with long arms and legs, resembling the white Scandinavian girls I used to see in rue de la Harpe, or rue Huchette, walking and clinging tightly to negroes with faces grey or so black that they were almost undistinguishable from the night.' He finds it a matter of surprise that 'the scenes between Titania and Bottom transformed into an ass are often played for laughs in the theatre'.

Even the Pyramus and Thisbe scenes weigh heavily upon him:

The theme of love will return once more in the old

tragedy of Pyramus and Thisbe, performed at the
end of the *Dream* by Master Quince's troupe. The
lovers are divided by a wall, cannot touch each
other and only see each other through a crack.
They will never be joined together. A hungry lion
comes to the rendezvous and Thisbe flees in panic.
Pyramus finds her blood-stained mantle and stabs
himself. Thisbe returns, finds Pyramus's body and
stabs herself with the same dagger. The world is
cruel for true lovers.

Kott on *A Midsummer Night's Dream* illustrates one
way in which an untheatrical reading of a play can produce a distorted critical image. Kott's failure of theatrical
imagination is the product of fantasy—of his use of the
text to release, in this case, extraordinary erotic and even
sadistic visions which he then attempts to impose on his
readers as an interpretation of the play.

Kott, then, uses the play as a stimulus to his own
imagination and, by selecting certain aspects of the text,
produces a bizarre falsification of it. Distortion may also
be the result of very serious and laudable attempts to
interpret the text as it is, but without sufficient regard
for the medium in which Shakespeare is working. A. C.
Bradley, in his *Shakespearean Tragedy*, discussing the
figure of Banquo, analyses his character and function with
scrupulous care and attention to the text. He claims that
'Shakespeare's intention' is 'frequently missed'. He finds
that Banquo 'may be described much more truly than
Macbeth as the victim of the witches'. He finds in the
Banquo of the first act, up to his and Duncan's arrival
at Macbeth's castle, 'that freedom of heart, and that
sympathetic sense of peace and beauty, which the Macbeth of the tragedy could never feel'. But at the beginning

of Act II Banquo has the speech starting:

> A heavy summons lies like lead upon me,
> And yet I would not sleep. Merciful powers
> Restrain in me the cursed thoughts that nature
> Gives way to in repose.

The 'cursed thoughts' could be either suspicions of what Macbeth may be intending to do, or temptations on his own account, or (as usual) both. Bradley takes them as temptations, though various later speeches show, as he admits, that Banquo is on the side of right—especially his reaction to the murder:

> In the great hand of God I stand, and thence
> Against the undivulged pretence I fight
> Of treasonous malice.

'He is', says Bradley, 'profoundly shocked, full of indignation, and determined to play the part of a brave and honest man.' But Bradley goes on to accuse Banquo of later giving way to temptation.

When next we see him, on the last day of his life,
we find that he has yielded to evil. The Witches
and his own ambition have conquered him. He alone
of the lords knew of the prophecies, but he has said
nothing of them. He has acquiesced in Macbeth's
accession, and in the official theory that Duncan's
sons had suborned the chamberlains to murder him.
Doubtless, unlike Macduff, he was present at Scone
to see the new king invested. He has, not formally
but in effect, 'cloven to' Macbeth's 'consent'; he is
knit to him by 'a most indissoluble tie'; his advice
in council has been 'most grave and prosperous';
he is to be the 'chief guest' at that night's supper.

And his soliloquy tells us why:

> Thou hast it now: King, Cawdor, Glamis, all
> As the weird women promised, and, I fear,
> Thou play'dst most foully for't: yet it was said
> It should not stand in thy posterity,
> But that myself should be the root and father
> Of many kings. If there come truth from them—
> As upon thee, Macbeth, their speeches shine—
> Why, by the verities on thee made good,
> May they not be my oracles as well,
> And set me up in hope?

And Bradley sees Banquo's death as a punishment for having 'kept his secret ... in order to make good *his* part of the predictions after Macbeth's own precedent'.

I think that Bradley's interpretation of Banquo is mistaken, and that his mistake is the result of attributing importance to something that Banquo does *not* do, or at least is not shown to do. We are simply never told whether or not he has discussed his suspicions with anyone else. It is not suggested that he should have done so, nor that he has any real knowledge that would have made him a plausible informer. I think that the reason Banquo stays with Macbeth is not that he wishes to take advantage of this position in order to further his own ends, but that Shakespeare needs to keep him alongside Macbeth in order for the dramatic design to be fulfilled. To speak of his death as a punishment for a crime is to make Macbeth an instrument of divine justice, which seems a curious and unwarranted mitigation of Macbeth's evil. Bradley is imposing on the play considerations that are irrelevant, that we are not invited to contemplate, and that would be unlikely to enter our minds in the theatre. In doing so he weakens our sense of Banquo as a representative of the stable, virtuous man, and diminishes the effect on Macbeth's conscience of the appearance of Banquo's ghost. Bradley is treating the words of the play as if they were the dialogue in a novel, and weaving his own authorial commentary around them. An actor could scarcely give the role the significance that he attributes to it. If Bradley had been studying the play primarily in the theatre he would have been unlikely to make this mistake.

To point to the danger of this kind of misreading is not, however, to suggest that the reading of plays is in any sense an illegitimate activity, or that we can hope to avoid the general necessity of studying drama on the page rather than in performance. Plays, especially Shakespeare's, have during the past century or so become a major instrument of education, in schools as well as universities. The scripts of plays are studied in great detail, and even if such study includes consideration of the plays in performance, and sometimes even preparation for performance, the verbal texture of the plays is bound to be a primary object of study. Nor is there anything intrinsically wrong about this situation. L. C. Knights, in his well-known essay 'How Many Children Had Lady Macbeth?', attacked the study of Shakespeare's plays as if they were novels, and asserted firmly, 'a Shakespeare play is a dramatic poem'. This is on the whole acceptable. We might be inclined to adjust the emphases and to assert that a Shakespeare play is above all a play; but we should not be likely to deny it the label of a poem, too.

Historically Professor Knights is likely to be classed among a school of critics who, reacting against those who approached the plays as if they were novels, have tended to overstress the play as poem. Each age needs to make its own readjustments of the critical picture. G. E. Bentley, in *Shakespeare and his Theatre* (1964), attacks those who write about the plays as if they were intended to be read. He inveighs especially against imagery study.

> Now all these fascinating studies of images, poetic symbols, and word patterns require a very careful and sensitive reading of the plays. Even a thoughtful and uninterrupted examination of the text from Act I, Scene i to the end of the play is generally not enough to understand the points made by so much modern criticism about the play; one must work backward and forward through the comedy or tragedy —from Act I to Act III, from Act IV back to Act II, from the climax back to the opening, from the denouement back to the rising action. Even the most perceptive playgoer could never take in these verbal patterns by the ear alone, and the students of imagery do not maintain that he could. They are studying Shakespeare the Poet, rather than Shakespeare the Playwright.

The trouble with this is that the final implied antithesis is false. Shakespeare the Poet is not antithetical to Shakespeare the Playwright; the first is an aspect of the second. To complain that the playgoer cannot during the course of the performance discern verbal subtleties to which a critic of imagery can point is like complaining that a concertgoer is unlikely during a performance to make a mental note of all the changes of key in a concerto. Subtleties are there whether we analyse them or not. They may work on us without our conscious recognition; this is what makes them subtleties. Sometimes lines of imagery lie very much on the surface of a play. It is not easy to think for long about *Henry IV, Part One*, without realizing that 'honour' is a key-word, and that the different uses of it by different characters, especially Hal, Hotspur, and Falstaff, form a significant part of the dramatic as well as the verbal pattern. On the other hand, some of Shakespeare's subtleties are very subtle indeed, and we owe our awareness of them to the critics whom Bentley criticizes. These critics, in studying the play as a poem, are often studying aspects of the play that are important in our subconscious apprehension of it even if without the critics' help we could not realize what was creating the effect we experienced. The mass of animal imagery, or of imagery relating to sight or to clothing, in *King Lear*, for example, is not what the average playgoer comes out of the theatre discussing; but it has certainly had its importance in the play's effect on him. When Professor Bentley attacks the study of play as poem he is in effect also attacking the study of poem as poem, since a conscious analysis of poetic devices is not an essential part of reading a poem, any more than of seeing a play. What is important in close study of the verbal structure of plays is that it should not lose sight of the fact that the play is a play. It would, for example, be false to write about the imagery of sight in *King Lear* without giving great prominence to the effect on the audience of the represented blinding of Gloster. This is the visual, physical outcrop of many verbal strata, and is overwhelming in its impact, so that the moment of Gloster's blinding cannot be considered as just one statistical counter. An unimaginative critic, reading the play purely as poem, might commit such an error; but this does not invalidate the kind of study in which he is engaged.

An attack such as Professor Bentley's represents a clear attempt to swing critical attention from one direction to another. As such it may be well justified; and some of the apparent philistinism in Professor Bentley's attitude may be the result of his feeling a need to jolt his hearers and readers out of a well-worn rut. In fact the trend in Shakespeare criticism at present is towards theatre-based studies. But the best critics of Shakespeare are those who speak of Shakespeare the Poet as well as Shakespeare the Playwright, just as the best producers of Shakespeare are those who give full weight to Shakespeare the Poet— Shakespeare the Dramatic Poet, of course—who was so important an aspect of Shakespeare the Playwright.

The interaction of criticism and performance

It will be apparent that I do not believe in a clear division between literary and theatrical approaches to Shakespeare. Theatrical experience of the plays is necessary for a Shakespeare critic, and the writings of Shakespeare critics can perform a valuable service to the theatre, both in their direct influence on producers and actors, and also in their influence on the theatregoing public. The influence is not always good. But informed and serious close study of the plays and their backgrounds is a necessary accompaniment to serious attempts to stage the plays—at least if the attempt is to stage the plays in themselves rather than to use them as raw material for the creative impulses of directors. The theatre has always displayed a tendency to simplify Shakespeare. So, in their ways, have academic critics; but at least their ways have been different ways. The critic—the reader of the plays —is faced with a complete text; in the theatre we often see considerably less. The theatre will often pare the play down towards its basic story line, shortening it either by omitting entire scenes or by that kind of cutting which is known as internal—the reduction of a speech in a way that simplifies its syntax and stresses the content rather than the manner. This fact in itself points to a characteristic of Shakespeare: that his plays include a good deal of verbal elaboration that is not essential to the narrative line. Often enough he could have told substantially the same story in considerably fewer words. Some of his plays are exceptionally long by any standards. We may doubt whether *Hamlet*, *King Lear*, and *Antony and Cleopatra*, to take a few examples, were ever performed complete in their own day. They are longer than most plays by other, contemporary dramatists, and than most of Shakespeare's other plays. In them he seems to have indulged himself. Perhaps his company and his public indulged him in turn, realizing that he was exceptional. More probably his plays were cut in his day just as they have been cut ever since. But the fact remains that to shorten a work of art is to alter it. One of the functions that critics can perform is to show the relevance to a play of passages that are inessential to its story line. Sometimes such passages are, luckily, so striking that no one is likely to remove them. An example is the Dover Cliff scene between mad Lear and blind Gloster. It contributes nothing to the story of the play; yet who would dispute its importance? But many passages that can be shown to be important in the design of their play have, at one time or another, been traditionally omitted. Throughout the nineteenth century, *Hamlet* regularly ended with Hamlet's dying words—'The rest is silence.' It was. Beerbohm Tree prided himself on preserving an additional couple of lines out of the forty-four which follow in the complete text. He wrote:

> Kissing the forehead of his friend, and with his father's picture on his heart, Hamlet says, with his last breath,

> The rest is silence.

Here as a rule the curtain falls in silence, but I prefer to preserve Horatio's beautiful words:

> Now cracks a noble heart. Good-night, sweet Prince,
> And flights of angels sing thee to thy rest.

His curtain fell with, as he puts it, 'the faint echo of heavenly music ringing in our ears'—in other words, a celestial chorus in the wings.

It was with Forbes-Robertson's production in 1897 that the play's closing lines began to appear in the theatre, provoking Shaw's famous review beginning:

> The Forbes-Robertson *Hamlet* at the Lyceum is,
> very unexpectedly at that address, really not at all
> unlike Shakespear's play of the same name. I am
> quite certain I saw Reynaldo in it for a moment; and
> possibly I may have seen Voltimand and Cornelius;
> but just as the time for their scene arrived, my eye
> fell on the word 'Fortinbras' in the programe, which
> so amazed me that I hardly know what I saw for
> the next ten minutes.

(It is one of the nicer ironies of theatre history that Professor W. A. Armstrong has been able to show that in fact Shaw himself exerted influence on the production, so that the surprise expressed in his review should not be taken too seriously.)

Now that Shakespeare is no longer a popular dramatist in the sense that he was till perhaps forty years ago, extensive cutting is less common than it used to be. But barbarous cuts are still made even in fairly short plays. The prompt-book of Peter Hall's production of *A Midsummer Night's Dream* at Stratford in 1959 reveals the omission of, for example, most of Titania's speech beginning 'These are the forgeries of jealousy', the beautiful awakening into reality of the lovers after their magic night, and Hippolyta's reply to Theseus's speech on imagination. The story of the play can, it is true, be conveyed without these passages, and the Venus de Milo would still be recognizable if you sliced off her nose, but neither alteration ought to be considered an improvement. Shakespeare was writing poetic drama, and his method implied a willingness on the part of his audience to listen to speeches which reveal the drama of intelligence and poetry rather than of physical action. Shakespeare was a dramatist of ideas as well as of story and character, and to reduce his ideas is to diminish his plays. The critic who draws attention to the ideas, even if he does so at the expense of more obviously theatrical ingredients, does something to redress a balance which may be in danger of being lost.

While academic study is necessary to the health of the theatre, the critics too need to learn from the stage. The lessons they can learn are both specific and general. They can learn, that is, once they have seen particular plays, to give proper importance to the theatrical impact of moments in those plays which might otherwise seem insignificant or underwritten. I referred in the first chapter to such moments as the entry of the messenger of death in *Love's Labour's Lost*, or the final entry of Katharina in *The Taming of the Shrew*. They may be helped, too, in more general terms, to recognize potentially effective theatrical qualities even in plays they have not seen. They may, indeed, learn to value the quality that we may call 'theatricality', that is, the revelation of an imagination that works in terms of spectacle, movement, even music and dance, as well as through words. This is not, of course, an undiscriminating quality. Truly theatrical effects need to be as skilfully controlled as purely verbal ones. A play that seemed to me to use supposedly theatrical effects in an unsuccessful manner is Peter Shaffer's *The Royal Hunt of the Sun*, which was produced by the National Theatre in London. I went to see this play with expectations of a thrilling theatrical experience. The play itself had not been greatly admired, but the production had been highly praised for its supposedly theatrical qualities. When I saw it, I felt how false was the division implied by such praise. I found that the play had only a low level of interest. It seemed to me little more than a series of semi-didactic, semi-philosophical dialogues with no real drama of action, character, or thought. Admittedly, every so often there was a dance, a passage of mime, or an unusual lighting effect; but these all seemed to me to be extraneous effects applied in the attempt to give interest to a thin script.

On the other hand, similar methods may be used with complete success to reinforce a script which may be to a greater or lesser degree dependent on them. Trevor Nunn's production of *The Revenger's Tragedy*, first given by the Royal Shakespeare Company in 1967, may be taken as an example, and is indeed especially useful because it included instances of three different kinds of theatrical effect: those which, however effective in themselves, may seem extraneous; others which are a legitimate but inessential reinforcement of the text; and others which represent an effective theatrical realization of a necessary part of the action only lightly sketched in by the author. An inserted mime at the beginning of the play, showing the rape of Antonio's wife, comes in the first category. It was good theatre but inessential to the play's total impact, as is shown by the fact that it was omitted when the production was first given. As an instance of legitimate but inessential reinforcement of the text I would cite the decision to play one scene of unlocalized dialogue in a fencing school, and another in a torture chamber. And as an example of admirable realization of effects required but not fully specified by the author I would cite the beginning of Act V, Scene iii, where in the printed text we have the stage direction: '*In a dumb show, the possessing of the young Duke with all his nobles; then sounding music.*' The direction indicates that the author envisaged some kind of spectacle, doubtless a way of impressing on the audience in a wordless scene that Lussurioso is now Duke, but he did not specify the details. In performance, the simple instruction was superbly realized in an episode in which the young Duke and his court, clad in the black and silver that had been used throughout the production, marched in slow and ritualistic fashion, their backs to the audience, the stiff fabric of their robes swishing sinisterly with each obscene thrusting forth of their bodies, till the unworthy Duke mounted his throne in corrupt splendour. Still more effective, as episodes which are integral to the play's action, were those presenting the masques of revengers in the final scene, where the producer is required to realize in stage terms the direction '*The revengers dance*'. A cleverly devised mime of masked figures bearing swords and dancing to the insistent rhythm of an off-stage drum created an appropriate tension before the multiple killings which form the climax of the action.

These theatricalities are those of the director, episodes devised by him and executed by his performers. Another aspect of the theatrical which may be calculated by the author and for which the critic should make allowance is the virtuosity of the actor. Shakespeare, we know, was writing for a particular company, and must have known that at times he could leave something to his performers. A dramatist who does this takes a risk. If he relies on the clown who can set the table on a roar by his appearance alone and therefore fails to write for him dialogue that has comic merit in its own right, he cannot expect to be admired by posterity. But though he cannot always have the actors of his choice, he has the right to hope that his plays will be intelligently cast, that his actors will be suited to their roles, and that they will bring to them something of their own personal qualities. And the critic needs to make sympathetic allowance for such expectations.

In this, as in so many other matters, the critic needs to use his imagination; and he needs to allow for the fact that other people's imaginations may work in ways different from his own. A play has no constant reality; it changes from performance to performance, still more from production to production. This is a situation that should be accepted and even rejoiced in. But the theatre is more liable to take this view than the academic critic. Theatrical producers tend to seek for novelty, to be constantly on the watch for new ways of presenting classical works. It is, within limits, a laudable aim. A stereotyped repetitiveness in production methods of plays could have nothing but a harmful effect. Constant experimentation and adaptation to changing circumstances is desirable as well as inevitable. It results, from time to time, in excess. It results in productions which, we may feel, exploit plays rather than interpreting them—productions such as Zeffirelli's of *Much Ado About Nothing*, and Tyrone Guthrie's of *All's Well that Ends Well*.

But it results also in serious attempts to interpret the plays in different ways. In 1967, for instance, two productions of *As You Like It* were simultaneously on show in London. One, by the Birmingham Repertory Theatre, was given in modern dress with, for example, Touchstone as a kind of hotel page-boy. The other, by the Royal Shakespeare Company (revived in 1968), was performed in traditional costumes and with the kinds of sets that have resulted from the influence of studies in the Elizabethan theatre upon the pictorial tradition of the nineteenth century. Each production was susceptible to criticism upon a number of points, but each also was a serious attempt to put across a valid interpretation of the play. Each demanded to be judged in its own terms rather than measured, point for point, against the other.

The openness of interpretation implicitly claimed by the theatre is something that needs to be recognized too by those who write about Shakespeare. Critics as well as producers can exploit him for their own ends. Kott's essay on *A Midsummer Night's Dream* is a personal fantasy vaguely based on the play, just as some productions have been; and Kott writes at length of *King Lear* without mentioning Cordelia. But critics can write in very different ways about a play without contradiction or falsity. Studies of imagery, of characters, studies of the text in relation to its stage history, studies of ideas, themes, and morality, of narrative and dramatic conventions, of historical or social background—these are all valid approaches that may yield different but equally valuable results. What none of them is likely to do is to arrive at any absolute and final truth, except perhaps on matters of detail. It is no accident that the drama, especially Shakespeare, has been more productive of critical writing than other literary forms. It is a fact that we may deplore as we face row upon row of critical books on Shakespeare. But it is natural and understandable, considering the medium in which he was working. It is, I have stressed, an imprecise medium. It is highly productive of ambiguity. It requires collaboration— collaboration on the part of those who perform the plays, and also on the part of those who read them. The quality and kind of collaboration vary from performer to performer, and from reader to reader. Each brings to the plays different responses, different knowledge, different powers of imagination. Each therefore takes away from the plays a different impression and, if he writes about them, does so in different terms, from a different point of view, and creates a different image.

Shakespeare's special quality

This is liable to be true of plays in general, but particularly of Shakespeare, because Shakespeare is so rich, so dense in texture, so 'myriad-minded' (in Coleridge's phrase), that he is quite peculiarly elusive and therefore open to variety of interpretation. This might seem a limitation, as if he had not completely expressed himself, and indeed it has seemed so to those who require their works of art to be cut and dried, to have a readily definable meaning, to make clear-cut demands of the reader. One of the most elusive of all the plays has been *Hamlet*—at least it has seemed so since the late eighteenth century. Yet it has remained intensely exciting and popular, and when T. S. Eliot in a moment of exasperation referred to it as 'an artistic failure' he may well have been influenced by the play's resistance to analysis and clear-cut interpretation. It is just this, it seems to me, which is responsible for its continuing vitality. Peter Hall, taking on the role of critic before he gave his production of *Hamlet*, wrote well about it when he said '*Hamlet* is one of mankind's great images. It turns a new face to each century, even to each decade. It is a mirror which gives back the reflection of the age that is contemplating it.' And referring the play to the theatre he went on, 'there is never an ideal production of *Hamlet*; any interpretation must limit'. If Shakespeare is, in Ben Jonson's phrase, 'for all time', this is partly because he demands the collaboration of those who submit themselves to him—demands not merely intelligence of response, such as is demanded by, for instance, *Paradise Lost*, or *Middlemarch*, but demands a more creative response, and demands it from the reader as well as the performer. Again this is to some extent a feature of the medium in which he was working. Compare, for example, a play with a film. A film is fixed, determined. Like a play, it is a collaborative product; but the collaboration is simultaneous, and once it has occurred it is over. A film, like a naturalistic painting, is closed, final, of its age, a period piece. But plays go on growing and developing. They are capable of having a life of their own.

To say this is not to claim that the art of the playwright is necessarily a higher art than that of the poet, the novelist, or the film-maker. That would be absurd. But the works of Shakespeare owe something of their power to the fact that they are plays, and therefore have no finally defined form. They owe it too to the fact that they are so difficult to grasp in their totality. This is a complex effect, the result of both what is there and what is not there. What is there is difficult to grasp because it is so rich and full. The pattern of each play is not a single pattern but, as it were, a series of superimposed patterns so complexly interrelated that they can never finally be distinguished one from another. What is not there is difficult because it requires an exercise of the imagination. But the difficulty is something to rejoice in rather than to deplore. It means that the plays are stimulating to the imagination as well as satisfying; that they raise questions as well as answering them; that part of their meaning comes from those who experience them. This is one of the answers to the frequently posed question, 'Is there any point in going on writing about Shakespeare?' The plays will continue to be productive of new meanings as long as people continue to perform and to read them. No one will ever tell the final truth about them because there is no final truth to be told. To say this is not to say that a play has no self, that it lacks identity. It is not to say that we are entitled to read any meaning we like into a play. The dramatist presents us with a great deal of evidence, which we neglect at our peril. If there is no final truth, there are temporary ones which ask to be observed. The play can only really work on us, only really stretch our imagination, if we make an attempt to take it in, whole and entire. We need to try to take account of all the evidence, to understand all the words, to allow all the images to play against each other, because if we fail to do so, we shall be creating the play in our image rather than submitting ourselves to it. This is a common failing; and one reason why it is helpful to go on reading critics is that they may help to arouse our response to areas of the play of which we have not previously been aware. It is easy to make our own mental cuts during the reading of a play—to read mainly for plot, for instance—in a way that is not dissimilar from the treatment that plays often receive in the theatre.

Allowing for the necessary degree of imprecision in the theatrical medium, it seems clear that literary interpretations that claim to find in plays a clearly defined 'meaning' are likely to be misguided. A play is not, generally, an allegorical presentation of a philosophical proposition. Even if it is, it is likely to be less schematic than would an abstract statement of the same proposition. By presenting a simulation of human life in action, plays tend to suggest rather than to state meanings. The suggestion may be very strong. But always there is likely to be an unwritten dimension that can take different forms in the minds of a variety of readers and spectators. It is still possible for critics to argue that Hamlet ends his play in moral defeat rather than victory; that Macbeth in his final moments is merely the 'dead butcher' that Malcolm calls him; that Prospero is harshly tyrannical because he cannot forgive his brother. It is this unwritten dimension that should cause us to pause before making final pronouncements about the overall significance of theatrical writings. We may be quite sure about the significance they bear for us; and this may be worth stating; but there is danger in equating our response with the author's intention. This is a real justification for impressionistic criticism. The critic may point to objectively verifiable patterns in, for instance, the structure or the poetic imagery of a play. He may also, more creatively, write about the play's overall effect in relation to himself. The reacting personality is a necessary element in the critical process.

In the theatre the interpretative problem may seem greater. Whereas the literary critic may within a single essay express uncertainty, may suggest alternative interpretations or ambiguity of significance, the actor and director, it may appear, have to make up their minds. The actor playing Hamlet has to know whether he ends the play in hope or despair. There may be some truth in this, but the general argument of this book works towards a plea for openness of interpretation in the theatre as well as the study. This is not to say that plays can 'act themselves', any more than pieces of music can play themselves. It is to suggest that actors, like musicians, will be serving their author best if they can find a way of playing their parts that will stimulate variety rather than limitation of response. Of course, a single-minded interpretative performance may have value as a stimulus, just as a one-sided critical view may provoke thought more vigorously than a conventionally well-balanced one. Even as one says this one has to add that it assumes readers or spectators who are willing and able to take a comparative approach, who are interested enough to compare one interpretation against another. The most generally satisfactory productions of plays will be ones in which the audience is not conscious that a particular interpretation is being stressed. Hamlets who are self-consciously Oedipean, Othellos who attempt to portray homosexual overtones in their relationship with Iago, any production of any Shakespeare play which is visibly attempting to show that it is a Christian allegory: these are all bound to diminish the potential response and also to distort the play. A production in 1969 of *The Winter's Tale* gave great prominence to the 'theme' of time; it employed tricks of lighting to suggest that Leontes's jealousy was caused by schizophrenia; and it provided an objective correlative to his mental affliction after Hermione's apparent death by showing in him the symptoms of a stroke. As a result, it seemed to me, the play's poetic and emotional impact was weakened. The director assumed the role of commentator; and the result was not happy.

On the other hand, interpretative emphases which derive from a consistent use of clues given by the text may reveal previously unapprehended aspects of a play. Thus, in John Barton's 1969 production of *Twelfth Night*, we were unusually conscious that Sir Toby Belch's whole livelihood depended on the hospitality of his niece, Olivia, and on her toleration of his boorish behaviour. The crucial passage was one in the scene of midnight revelry, in which Sir Toby's confrontation with Malvolio was made to seem much more serious than it sometimes does. The tone is apparently light-hearted.

'Shall I bid him go and spare not?'

sings Sir Toby. Feste responds :

'Oh no, no, no, no, you dare not!'

This came as a real challenge, fiercely taken up.

Out o' tune, sir. Ye lie.

Sir Toby's wrath against Malvolio was the more impressive in that it was clear that he knew he was endangering his own position as he rounded on Malvolio with:

Art any more than a steward? Dost thou think,
because thou art virtuous, there shall be no more
cakes and ale?

There was at other points, too, the suggestion of a serious economic basis to the relationship between Sir Toby and Olivia, which extended also to his relationship with Maria and Sir Andrew Aguecheek. It contributed to an overall sombreness in the production, but it seemed an entirely justifiable result of a consistent and intelligent rethinking of the text. The production made a play different from any other *Twelfth Night* I had seen, but in ways that seemed to reveal a flexibility of interpretation inherent in the text itself, and thus to be broadening rather than limiting. It was an illustration, in fact, of the richness of great drama: of the fact that great plays are inexhaustible, and that we can constantly renew our appreciation of them by reading them, by reading about them, and by seeing them performed.

Bibliography

Below are listed writings cited in the text, with some suggestions for further reading.

Chapter 1

Byron's *Marino Faliero* is conveniently available in the second of the three volumes of his works in Everyman's Library (Dent), first issued in 1910. John Russell Brown's *Shakespeare's Plays in Performance* was published by Edward Arnold in 1966, and reprinted in the Penguin Shakespeare Library in 1969. Ann Jellicoe's *The Knack*, first performed in 1963, is published by Faber and Faber. Kenneth Tynan's piece on Sir Laurence Olivier as Coriolanus is included in *Tynan on Theatre* (Penguin Books, 1964), and Glynne Wickham's 'Coriolanus: Shakespeare's Tragedy in Rehearsal and Performance', from *Later Shakespeare*, Stratford-upon-Avon Studies 8, edited by J. R. Brown and B. Harris (Edward Arnold, 1966), is reprinted in his *Shakespeare's Dramatic Heritage* (Routledge and Kegan Paul, 1969). *The Bells* by Leopold Lewis is included in *Nineteenth Century Plays* edited by George Rowell (World's Classics, O.U.P., 1953). Gordon Craig's description of Irving in that play is from his *Henry Irving* (Dent, 1930). The quotation from Henry James on Irving is from an article first printed in 1880, and reprinted in *The Scenic Art* (Rupert Hart-Davis, 1949). Beerbohm's obituary of Dan Leno was reprinted in

Around Theatres (Rupert Hart-Davis, 1953). Granville-Barker's
'Preface' to *King Lear* appeared in 1927; the collected *Prefaces
to Shakespeare* were published in two volumes in 1958 (Batsford), and in four Batsford paper-back volumes with an introduction by Muriel St. Clare Byrne in 1963. T. S. Eliot's 'Poetry
and Drama', a lecture delivered in 1950, is in *Selected Prose*
(Penguin Books, 1953).

Chapter 2

T. S. Eliot's *The Cocktail Party* (1949) has been reprinted several
times by Faber and Faber. The play's evolution is revealingly
studied in *The Making of T. S. Eliot's Plays*, by E. Martin
Browne (Cambridge, 1969). An important study of early plays
relevant to this chapter is David Bevington's *From 'Mankind'
to Marlowe* (Cambridge, Mass., 1962), and basic scholarly information about them and later plays is to be found in W. W.
Greg's *A Bibliography of the English Printed Drama to the
Restoration* (4 volumes, Bibliographical Society, 1939-59), and
in Chambers's *The Elizabethan Stage* (4 volumes, Oxford, 1923).
Many of the plays referred to in this chapter are available in
Malone Society Reprints. Sir Edward Dering's account books
are studied in T. Lennam's article 'Sir Edward Dering's Collec-
tion of Play-Books, 1619-1624', *Shakespeare Quarterly* xvi
(Spring 1965). Arthur Brown's article referred to on page 40 is
in *Shakespeare Survey 17* (C.U.P., 1964). Douglas Bush's remark
quoted on page 44 is from *English Literature in the Earlier
Seventeenth Century 1600-1660* (1945, second edition 1962), a
volume of the Oxford History of English Literature. The
standard edition of Ben Jonson's works, is that prepared by
C. H. Herford and Percy and Evelyn M. Simpson (11 volumes,
Oxford, 1925-52). J. B. Bamborough's remark quoted on page
49 is from his British Council pamphlet *Ben Jonson*, published
by Longmans, Green and Co. (1959); Allardyce Nicoll's on
page 51 is from *English Drama: A Modern Viewpoint* (Harrap,
1968). Bernard Shaw's *Plays Unpleasant*, first printed in 1898,
are in the standard edition published by Constable.

Chapter 3

Ben Jonson's masques have been edited by Stephen Orgel (Princeton, 1969), and are also, of course, included in the Herford and Simpson edition. Jonson's *Pleasure Reconciled to Virtue and Lovers Made Men*, and also Campion's *The Lords' Masque*, are included in *A Book of Masques in Honour of Allardyce Nicoll*, edited by T. J. B. Spencer and Stanley Wells (Cambridge, 1967), which also includes extracts from Busino's account of *Pleasure Reconciled to Virtue*. The Shakespeare adaptations mentioned on page 84 are included in *Five Restoration Adaptations of Shakespeare*, edited by Christopher Spencer (Urbana, Illinois, 1965). Garrick's 'Ode' is reprinted in Martha Winburn England's *Garrick's Jubilee* (Ohio State University, 1964).

Chapter 4

James Smith has written a study called '*The Jew of Malta* in the Theatre' (*Christopher Marlowe*, edited by Brian Morris, Mermaid Critical Commentaries, Benn, 1968). Jan Kott's *Shakespeare Our Contemporary* was published in England by Methuen in 1964, with an enlarged second edition in 1967. A. C. Bradley's *Shakespearean Tragedy* first appeared in 1904; L. C. Knights's 'How Many Children Had Lady Macbeth?', which first appeared in 1933, is reprinted in his *Explorations* (Chatto and Windus, 1946). G. E. Bentley's *Shakespeare and his Theatre* (1964) is published by the University of Nebraska Press. The passage by Beerbohm Tree quoted on pages 101-2 is from *Thoughts and After-Thoughts* (Cassell, 1913). Shaw's review is reprinted in *Shaw on Shakespeare*, edited by Edwin Wilson (Cassell, 1962; Penguin Shakespeare Library, 1969). W. A. Armstrong's article 'Bernard Shaw and Forbes-Robertson's *Hamlet*' is in *Shakespeare Quarterly* xv (1964). T. S. Eliot's essay on Marlowe is in his *Selected Essays* (Faber and Faber, 1932) and *Elizabethan Dramatists* (Faber and Faber, 1963). F. P. Wilson's *Marlowe and the Early Shakespeare* was published by O.U.P. in 1953. Glynne Wickham's *Shakespeare's Dramatic Heritage* (1969) is published by Routledge and Kegan Paul.